THE YOUTH SPECIALTIES
HANDBOOK
FOR ◆ ◆ ◆
GREAT CAMPS
& RETREATS

D1207837

Zondervan/Youth Specialties Books

THE YOUTH SPECIALTIES
HANDBOOK
FOR ◆ ◆ ◆
GREAT CAMPS
& RETREATS

Chap Clark

ZondervanPublishingHouse
Grand Rapids, Michigan

A Division of HarperCollinsPublishers

The Youth Specialties Handbook for Great Camps and Retreats

Copyright © 1990 by Youth Specialties, Inc.

Youth Specialties Books, 1224 Greenfield Drive, El Cajon, California 92021, are published by Zondervan Publishing House, 1415 Lake Drive, S.E., Grand Rapids, Michigan 49506

Library of Congress Cataloging-in-Publication Data

Clark, Chap, 1954-
    The youth specialties handbook for great camps and retreats / by Chap Clark.
        p. cm.
    ISBN 0-310-57991-0
    1. Church camps. 2. Retreats for youth. 3. Youth—Religious life.
    I. Title.
BV1650.C52 1990
259'.23—dc20   90-32275
                                                               Rev. CIP

Edited by Cheri McLaughlin

Designed by Blue Water Ink

Printed in the United States of America

90 91 92 93 94 95 96 97 98 99 / DH / 10 9 8 7 6 5 4 3 2 1

About the YouthSource™ Publishing Group

YouthSource™ books, tapes, videos, and other resources pool the expertise of three of the finest youth-ministry resource providers in the world:

Campus Life Books—publishers of the award-winning *Campus Life* magazine, who for nearly fifty years have helped high schoolers live Christian lives.

Youth Specialties—serving ministers to middle-school, junior-high, and high-school youth for over twenty years through books, magazines, and training events such as the National Youth Workers Convention.

Zondervan Publishing House—one of the oldest, largest, and most respected evangelical Christian publishers in the world.

Campus Life
465 Gundersen Dr.
Carol Stream, IL 60188
708/260-6200

Youth Specialties
1224 Greenfield Dr.
El Cajon, CA 92021
619/440-2333

Zondervan
1415 Lake Dr., S.E.
Grand Rapids, MI 49506
616/698-6900

CONTENTS

ACKNOWLEDGMENTS

This book is not so much *my* contribution to youth ministry as it is the contribution of hundreds of others who taught me how to run Christian youth camps. I am indebted to every counselor, speaker, program director, property manager, and young person I have ever been with at a camp. Whether I met you in my teens at Young Life or at one of the camps, retreats, and conventions I've attended as an adult, you have taught me a great deal.

There are a few individuals, however, who deserve a specific word of thanks:

> **Kevin "Hoagy" Ayers**, one of the most loveable kids I have ever known, who was called home at 27 years of age, on September 13, 1990.
>
> **Bob Krulish**, my supervisor, mentor, and good friend, who has freed me up to follow God's call on my life and schedule.
>
> **Donn Dirckx**, the humblest of servants, who has taught me that it is possible to run an excellent camp and to care for people in the process.
>
> Our **"accountability board"** and our Koinonia group, who keep me in touch with the importance of being committed first to relationships and second to my ministry.
>
> And **several close friends**, who give so that Dee and I can pursue God's call on our lives.

I can no longer write a book without telling the world how grateful I am for my family—the **Carlsons**, **Clarks**, **Sweeneys**, and **Cromers**; for my wonderful sister, **Charlotte**; and of course our kids—**Chappie**, our little "lion cub"; **Robbie**, with his tender heart; and beautiful **Kaitlyn**, who has been blessed with her mother's heart and eyes; and for **Dee**, the most gifted, most gracious, and most compassionate woman I have ever met. I love you all—thanks for lending me to this project!

INTRODUCTION

I met Shawn when he showed up with some football buddies at our weekly club meeting. A boisterous freshman, Shawn obviously was also a leader. He participated enthusiastically in the singing and the skit and was especially attentive as I spoke. I knew I was going to like the kid.

That spring I decided it would be great for Shawn to go to camp with us. It would be the perfect opportunity for him to hear the Gospel in understandable terms and relate to other teenagers and adults on a deep level. And in the process, he would observe and experience something called *community* (being part of a group in which you feel welcome and necessary).

Convinced that God wanted Shawn at camp, I made him my primary ministry focus. I started spending hours upon hours with Shawn and his friends: we played football and basketball and went to the beach together. I talked nonstop about what an incredible time we would all have at Woodleaf, even though none of them had yet committed to going. I never really gave them any option—they were going, and I wasn't taking no for an answer!

When June arrived, Shawn and three of his buddies were as excited about Woodleaf as I was. They even talked another fifteen friends (mostly girls!) into going; and of the forty kids we ended up taking, twenty-nine were freshmen.

That August, 1981, our leadership team was part of a beautiful time in history—nearly every one of our students made a serious commitment to follow Christ. We became a community, a family, and Shawn became one of the leaders of our little body at Rolling Hills High School.

Over the next three years Shawn was a driving force in our outreach club, as well as being a star athlete, president of his church youth group, and president of his high-school senior class.

Since graduating from college, he is back in town, "wasting time" with high-school students in the name of Jesus—encouraging them to go to camp and to take a look at their Creator. Shawn still talks about Woodleaf and how God used that week at camp to change his life.

Pete making faces on the bus . . . Joy, on a Jet Ski, showing up all the guys . . . Joe cranking heavy metal just hours before meeting Christ . . . Sarah sharing about her abuse as a five-year-old . . . Hoagy sitting on the rock praying for the first time . . . Mike yelling in the van . . . Mary struggling with her Dad's alcoholism . . . Chip weeping for an hour after hearing the message of the cross for the first time.

My memories of camping with kids. Some painful, most filled with joy, all memorable. In my fifteen-plus years of youth ministry, the times of greatest impact have come when we were away from the comforts of home. Looking back, my best memories were seldom program related. The van and bus rides—a headache I always want to avoid at the outset, but always a rich relational experience in the end. Those afternoons by the pool or lake, talking over a Coke, taking a walk, or just hanging around the cabin. I love going to camps and retreats with kids, because it is in those environments that hearts seem to melt and façades fall away.

For many of us, however, it is easy to forget those times. When we plan our camps and retreats, we work so hard at the logistics and at fine-tuning the camp's physical aspects that we often overlook the ones we are trying to touch.

The basic premise of this book is that camping and retreat programs are tools we can use to meet the needs of adolescents; they are not important in themselves. So often youth workers plan, organize, and operate camps in certain ways simply because "they've always worked that way." Instead, we should be asking how we can best use this exciting opportunity to best care for our students.

It is my conviction that the greatest things we can offer students are Jesus Christ and relationships. All the thrills and frills, all the programming, all the plans, all the studies and discussions, all the fun and teaching, should point kids to a deeper knowledge of Christ, to a safe environment where community thrives, and to opportunities for authentic friendships with adults who care. Camping programs allow us time to build relationships and platforms of trust from which we can share the truths of the Christian faith.

This book can serve as a resource manual for *anyone* who prepares camps and retreats for adolescents. It is designed to help groups plan programs based on their kids' needs and to avoid the traditional "We've always done it this way" mentality. When we care enough for our students to produce camps and retreats that reach them at their points of need, we will be able to focus our time and energies where they belong—on thinking about, praying for, and spending time with our flock. May this book help you do a better job of loving kids.

SCRATCHING WHERE THEY ITCH

Camps and Retreats Designed to Meet Your Kids' Needs

SECTION ONE

SCRATCHING
WHERE THEY
ITCH

✦ ✦ ✦

Groups and Rentals
Designed to Meet
Your Kids' Needs

I n the fall of 1988, during the annual Youth Specialties National Youth-
worker's Convention, I was asked to do a seminar titled "Great Ideas
for Camps and Retreats." I heard lots of comments like, "We need
more of this"; "My kids seem to be tired of the same old retreats";
and, "Our denominational convention isn't hitting kids where they are;
what do you guys at Youth Specialties suggest?" This book was born
as a result of the responses given at that seminar.

As I thought, prayed, and researched, I came to the following
conclusion: In the thirty years that youth ministries have existed, our
presuppositions and philosophies about camps, retreats, and conferences have not kept up with the times. Even *parachurch* ministries—
which are actually expressions of the local church and not really *para*
(alongside of) at all, and which have historically had a stronger emphasis
on camping than most parish ministries—have been using pretty much
the same programs and philosophies for the past several decades.

Dressing Up a Dinosaur

To be sure, every youth ministry has worked hard to perfect and
refine its models—more programs, more hype, louder music, more
video—but there are just so many ways to dress up a dinosaur! In light
of the incredible changes that have taken place in the adolescent society
and in our homes and schools, I have come to the conclusion that we
are struggling to improve an animal that should have died out a long
time ago—the conventional retreat.

As diverse as youth ministries are across the globe, in North
America almost every denomination, organization, and church body
has maintained the same camping style and philosophy for many years.
Granted, it may look different from group to group, but the tendency
to hold on to history and tradition is common. (Maybe, in the name
of creativity, we could all simply swap programs with each other for
a decade or so—at least we would be forced to rethink our styles and
biases!) To make an impact on the adolescents of the nineties and
beyond, we must depart from our traditional courses and move into
uncharted waters to reach kids today.

I can hear the screams from here—"But it's working; why change
it?"

As our culture changes and the needs of young people change,
we need to change with them. Even if something works today, can we

be sure that it is working as well as it possibly can? And, more important, what guarantee do we have that it will work tomorrow?

Perhaps the greatest reason for rethinking our attitudes about camping and retreats is that the temptation to rely on our skills rather than on the Holy Spirit's leadership and intervention is far greater when we are working with a proven commodity. Risks draw us to our knees, and that is where every youth-ministry program must begin.

A Call to Risk

Does a call to risk mean that the basic elements of traditional camping like singing, skits, and games must be eliminated? Not at all! Traditional ingredients are valuable tools and structures that help create a quality experience. To build a revolutionary car for the nineties, we need not do away with the steering wheel or tires; it is the hidden layout of the steering mechanism and the structural design of the tires that may need changing. And when we reexamine a camping program in light of the needs of a given group of kids, we may not change our basic components at all. What *should* change is the planning, prayer, forethought, and intention of the overall camping experience. In other words, rather than concern ourselves with what tools to use, we need to concern ourselves with *how* and *why* we use them.

The purpose of this book is to help those responsible for youth camping programs to create experiences that meet the needs of their kids. The whys and hows of doing this will be discussed at length, for each is necessary.

Over the past twenty to thirty years of youth ministry, we have made great strides in learning what it means to provide kids with quality camping experiences. It would be wrong to throw out everything we've learned. Yet my challenge for you is to prayerfully analyze and carefully consider your kids' needs.

In applying the suggestions and philosophies presented in this book, your camps, retreats, and conferences may not look much different on the outside, but they will contain fresh and culturally relevant ingredients that will enhance your effectiveness. Therefore, this book is not so much a how-to manual as it is a resource for training and equipping youth workers to use the tool of camping to bring adolescents into an encounter with Jesus Christ and the church.

How to Use This Book

Great Camps and Retreats is divided into three sections. The first section is an overview of the elements that ensure successful and life-changing experiences for today's young people—from philosophical questions on the subjects of dancing and appropriate humor, to very practical advice on how to lead songs and divide up organizational responsibilities. Section One is practical enough to provide clear insight into the current cultural and sociological needs of kids and yet not be so confining that it excludes use by any organization or group. For example, denominational leaders responsible for a large youth conference can use the information just as well as youth ministers from small rural churches or seasoned staff members with Youth for Christ.

Section Two contains practical applications that groups can utilize when they decide what kind of a camp their kids need. At the beginning of Section Two ("Hitting Your Target") is a list of possible camping purposes—or visions—and the types of camps and retreats that will aid in accomplishing each purpose. For example, if a group decides they need a camp that will build community, they can refer to the list of purposes, locate the one dealing with community-building, and find which types of camps and retreats will aid its development.

Each of the chapters in Section Two is specific in its focus and purpose and will help youth leaders give their students the retreat or camping experiences most suited to their needs. Each chapter also includes specific goals or action plans, options unique to the type of camp being discussed, and a suggested schedule. These chapters are not provided as "instant retreats," where you "add kids and stir"! They are presented as foundations on which unique experiences can be built. Most of the information will need modification to fit your program, staff, and resources, but each chapter will give you enough information to get started, and that is the goal of Section Two.

Section Three contains information that is extremely helpful in developing a well-rounded understanding of effective camping in today's youth environment. The four appendices found there are referred to throughout the book, but because three of the four are excerpts from other works, they can also be read and used independently.

The Best We Can Offer

As you read *Great Camps and Retreats*, you may realize that the best gift we can offer the precious kids God has given to us is *relationships*—with Christ and other believers. Whatever we do with students in our camps, retreats, and conferences, let's always help them build relationships that are authentic and lasting and show them that they are valuable and worth our investment of time and energy. As we do, the Holy Spirit will have more freedom to reign in our kids' lives, because they will understand how deeply they are loved. May God bless you as you love your kids by giving every opportunity, and *especially* your camping and retreat opportunities, your very best shot.

1

Isn't It Time We Counterattacked?

L ast spring while I was at a camp with some friends, I heard a few of the leaders talking about the coming year. The discussion centered on topics like who they were going to get to perform musically, what type of media they were going to use, and who was going to speak. I couldn't resist.

"You're thinking about next year already?" I asked.

"We are late as it is! We usually book almost two years in advance, especially for musicians and speakers. We have been doing this for years," they replied.

"Have you been using the same basic philosophy and program all those years?"

"Of course. 'If it ain't broke, don't fix it!' We have had great success for almost fifteen years with this camp, so why should we bother changing it?"

I wanted to say, "Because kids have changed drastically over the past fifteen years, that's why. Shouldn't we begin thinking differently to keep up with them?" but I didn't. I didn't want to criticize a group of youth leaders who were no less cutting edge than ninety-five percent of their peers in North American youth work.

I did silently wonder, however, how often people in charge of youth groups, denominational youth programs, youth conventions, and retreat centers, take the time to ask certain fundamental questions about their plans—like, "Are we doing these things to meet the needs of today's kids?" Or, put another way, "Is what we're doing the *best* way to minister to the kids of the nineties?" Is it possible that most retreats, camps, and conferences are repeated year in and year out simply for tradition's sake? Are we so locked into the safety and security of past successes that we automatically discount any need to "go back to the drawing board" with our philosophies and programs?

I do not intend to offend, for I believe that nearly everyone operates in the safe way, especially when it comes to large and traditional programs. I *do*, however, mean to question the presuppositions that make us do what we do.

Have youth leaders ever stopped to wonder, as they proudly announce to their youth groups or Sunday school classes about the "Incredible Twelfth Annual Snow Camp," what that first camp was like? Its program was probably pretty shaky. I am relatively certain that the speaker stank and the music was worse. You can bet they lost a fortune, kids were flaky when it came to signing up, sponsors were reluctant and skeptical, boards asked some hard questions, and its organizers were sweating every minute. But I am also quite sure that there was a lot of prayer, reliance on the graciousness of the Holy Spirit, camaraderie, laughter, and satisfaction as the event progressed. Kids were touched in unique ways that met their needs from a fresh perspective; this was real "cutting-edge stuff."

The second year was a little more polished. The third and fourth cemented the schedule and expectations. Now, well into the second decade, the initiators are long gone, taking their creative edge with them. Today everyone likes the camp. The adults love the control that comes with time-honored traditions, and the kids seem to enjoy themselves. But in the midst of the twelfth season of preparation, has anyone stopped to ask, "Is this camp still the most effective programming tool I can use to bring my students closer to Christ? Or, has it outlived its usefulness, however relevant it once was?"

It is a rare, brave soul who asks that question. As I've already stated, there are some great advantages to years of experience with a camp or retreat. Logistical concerns like housing and meals, games and events that work best in a given facility, and topics or programs that never fail to attract kids—all improve over time.

The intent of my challenge to rethink every camp and retreat from the ground up is not to ignore lessons learned from history. The goal is to make sure that every tool and program we use meets today's kids where they live. It is likely that group singing is the best possible way to facilitate community building and interest in the speaker, for example; and, for most programs, group singing hasn't been tampered with much over the past several years.

But it is equally likely that as time has passed, there has been less commitment to *quality* group singing due to an inadvertently heightened commitment to musical performances and entertainment. In the case of the twelve-year-old snow camp, the program planners may need to reemphasize group singing in order to meet the needs of their group.

The philosophy of creating every camp or retreat as if it is a once-in-a-lifetime experience is important, because for many kids, that's what it will be.

Think of yourself as a painter preparing to create a masterpiece; you place on and around your easel all the tools of your trade—canvas, paints, and brushes. You ponder your subject, and, as is the case with so many of history's greatest artists, pause to pray for divine guidance and blessing. As you paint, each stroke is new, fresh, and unique. You may be using the colors and brushes from your last project, and maybe even the same model or landscape, but the picture itself is a new creation.

As you go to the drawing board with each camp, keep close to the tricks and tools of the trade—singing, humor, games, discussion, interactive and didactic teaching methods—and don't be afraid to use them. But keep in the forefront of your thoughts and prayers the importance of allowing the Holy Spirit and your kids' needs to dictate the use of those tools as your masterpiece is being created.

When tradition is challenged and youth leaders have the insight to program what is *needed* rather than what works or "what's always been done," the results will be undeniable. The lives of both students and leaders will be changed. Programs may be weak; there may be dissent in the ranks; but youth groups can't help but be healthier.

It is essential for us to understand our adolescents' needs. While there is no way to accurately and individually categorize every young person, there are some trends and universal needs: Every person needs time for interaction and discussion; every one needs the opportunity to know and experience a loving community; each individual needs to feel like a "star" and a "key kid"; and people all need to refocus on the heart of the Gospel, Jesus Christ.

The Need for Interaction and Discussion

As culture has become more and more impersonal, technologically dependent, and relationally independent, the means by which adolescents relate to others also has changed. The breakup of the family, the number of hours parents spend at work and with hobbies that take them away from home, and the media invasion have left kids with no one to talk to. What we used to refer to as "family rooms" have become entertainment centers. Families once treasured the dinner hour as a time for conversation; today they rarely even eat together—and when they do, it is in front of "Wheel of Fortune"! Our kids are growing up with few opportunities to interact with others on meaningful levels.

Young people all need to be known and to know others, even though many of them resist this truth and few understand it. We are social creatures who cannot stand to be without company. But kids today have been raised as if they need *no one*! They have been taught through such societal deities as the "miracle" of television that what is entertaining is worth knowing, and what doesn't keep their interest is useless, and this conditioning has affected their relationships. "Entertain me and I'm happy, but only for a time. Bore me and I'm gone."

When it comes to planning camps and retreats, many of us attempt to compete with the entertainment field. We try to "wow" our kids with fancier electronics, louder music, and flashier speakers. For them to get anything out of the event, we think we must entertain them. Despite the bombardment of cultural biases, we need to hold on to what we know is true—that because we are made in the image of the Creator of relationships, we all are desperate to have our thoughts, words, and feelings taken seriously.

I am not saying that we should abandon all attempts to entertain; in fact, I believe that our programs should be first-class, fun, and creative. But relying on technology and creativity to touch kids' lives is a mistake. While programming and gadgets are fine, we must always remember that they are simply tools with which to facilitate relationships. Once adolescents are given freedom to know and be known, and relationships are established, we must work overtime to put away the tools that got us there. They have served their purpose.

In practice it is easy to build in opportunities for interaction. I strongly recommend creating a *cabin family* to enable relationships to take hold. In these cabin groups, kids not only live together, but also work and play together and participate as a unit in competitive and group activities. Living with each other, sharing informal and programmed discussions, and simply experiencing the weekend or week of camp together, combine to break down barriers and build trusting friendships that last.

Other ideas for giving campers opportunities for interaction and discussion are small groups that meet regularly (i.e., daily before breakfast), or even small groups that meet in the middle of a general session. The more chances we give kids to talk and share their thoughts, opinions, and feelings, the more they are going to be influenced.

The Need for a Loving Community

Our society openly measures success and worth by performance. Mercy is rare in our world, and there is no sanctuary for the loser. We feel okay when we do well but are devastated when we fail. Even in our homes, which are supposed to be places of safety and comfort, many adolescents feel less loved and thus less valuable when they fail to meet their own expectations or the expectations of family members. Today, more than ever, youth ministries must provide the warmth, comfort, and security of a loving community, because for many young people, they will get it nowhere else.

The issue of meeting adolescents' community needs is broader than the scope of camps and retreats. But because this need is so great and because many of our kids are so lonely, we must use the great potential of camps to begin filling that need. For most kids, the suggestions I made about providing time for student discussion will fill the need for a loving community.

But community goes deeper than talking to a friend; it is knowing that we will be accepted and loved no matter what we do. Unconditional love is the foundation of community, and that love manifests itself as much in follow-up as it does during the retreat. As we give kids opportunities to build authentic love relationships during our camps, they will get a glimpse of what a community can be.

The Need To Feel Like a "Star"

I was raised on the philosophy of the *key kid*. This philosophy is based on missions experience—if you want to reach a village, reach the chief first; then the chief will help you reach the rest of the village. Now that is a very sound, strategic theory with which to reach *most* cultures. But many youth workers have struggled with how that theory works in practice. When we strategically go after key kids, *everybody* knows that is exactly what we're doing—the key kids know it, and the not-so-key kids know it.

In other words, this philosophy of ministry is socially hierarchical and suggests just the opposite of what Jesus would suggest or do. Second, while many youth groups function with a key-kid or student-leader methodology, the original intent of this philosophy was for use in evangelism, not discipleship! So what was proposed as a strategic theory for evangelism has somehow been adopted as standard procedure in youth ministry.

In a culture where far more adolescents feel like losers than winners, fewer and fewer key kids can be found. The real challenge of youth ministry in the coming decades is to convince young people that they are *all* stars! Some will never believe us, but each of them should be given the opportunity to know that we love them very much and that God does too.

We can do a great deal in a camp setting to help students build self-esteem. For example, competition has been a staple of Christian youth camping for years. But all too often, these competetive events are *individual* athletic contests that allow those who star at school to also star at camp. Why not restructure our competitions to enable some of those who never win at anything to come out on top? Events like relay races, which require whole-team participation, put everyone on equal footing. Others, like fishing derbies or contests for the most creative outfit, the best compliment, or the joke of the week, permit students who may never have had any recognition to stand out.

Students will also feel good about themselves when the camp staff and leaders treat them with respect and congeniality. Camp speakers should not be hidden professionals who never see the kids except when giving their talks. They are instantly admired by every camper and should use their status to make kids feel special. Sitting with students at meals, learning their names, and hanging out with those who need extra attention should be on the list of speaker expectations.

The same goes for the rest of the leaders—the ways that camp staff, leaders, and even key kids reach out does wonders to convince needy young people that they are important.

The Need to Refocus on the Person of Christ

Frank Peretti, in writing *This Present Darkness* and *Piercing the Darkness*, has done a great service to the church by reminding us that spirits exist and are waging battles over souls, a reality affirmed by Ephesians 6:12. In discussing the needs of kids as they enter the 1990s, we must not forget that our students' deepest and most pressing need is to come to know Jesus personally. I am not talking about a one-time shot, where someone can say they "did it" at camp when they were seven years old and moved on to a higher spiritual plane. The essence of the Christian faith is learning what it means to know, love, follow, and serve Jesus Christ.

Because this essence may seem so basic and elementary, especially for those students who have been in church all their lives, we tend to glorify service and effort as we lead students. Wishing to serve others is tremendous, and in the attempt to inflame this desire, many leaders and speakers have made it the focus of their ministry and messages. The danger lies, however, in the possibility that recruited students will serve simply for the sake of serving. Christian service, on the other hand, is by definition an internal call flowing from a heart committed to knowing and following Christ. If we focus on the person of Jesus and encourage students to respond to him, they will develop a servant's attitude spontaneously as they acquire the heart of Christ.

Whether a retreat is filled with solid Christian students who have been around for years or a thousand pagan kids, the need they will all share in common will be to hear the refreshing words of Christ and how he relates to their lives. They don't need prodding, guilt, or even exhortations to change from the inside; they need Jesus. The words of the apostle Paul are as important today as they were to his audience long ago:

> The god of this age has blinded the minds of unbelievers, so that they cannot see the light of the Gospel of the glory of Christ, who is the image of God. For we do not preach ourselves, but Jesus Christ as Lord, and ourselves as your servants for Jesus' sake (2 Corinthians 4:4–5) .◆

2

Developing a Camping Strategy

A youth pastor called recently and invited me to speak at a camp. I asked him, "What do you see as the purpose of the time?"

"What do you mean?"

"Well, what do you want to accomplish?"

"Oh, what we *always* want to accomplish! We need you to challenge our leadership kids to full-time service, be energetic enough to attract our disinterested kids, not be too heavy for those who are new to the group, and use a lot of Bible for the kids who need meat. But don't read too much—some kids will be bored before they arrive, and . . ."

This shotgun approach to camping, which aims to wound everyone, but actually does very little lifelong damage, is the norm for most church-related retreats. We often do what we do because we loved it when *we* did it in high school, or because we feel that it's important to please every kid (or at least not *offend* any of them). So we attempt to build a program that meets every need of every person we can think of—to challenge those who are ready to be challenged, and to entertain and soothingly entice those who are not. But is this the most effective way to run a camping ministry? The premise of this book is that we must be purposeful with the gift of time a retreat or camp provides.

John Westerhoff, a leader in modern Christian education, once said that to be really effective we should eliminate Sunday schools and use the money spent on them for camps and retreats. He believes that getting everybody in a church away for two weekend retreats a year is more effective than a year's worth of hour-long Sunday-school classes.

We have few opportunities to remove people from everyday life and focus their attentions completely on community building. Kids (and adults) are incredibly busy—so busy that regular attendance at weekly meetings is often impossible. But many *will* make time for a retreat. To be effective, we must think through these unique times with people and keep our planning purposeful. Without a clear vision and specifically defined goals, it is very difficult to make spiritual progress with those we are called to lead.

For any program, and especially any camping program, to be effective, we must follow a three-step process: We must develop a *vision*, set *goals*, and carefully formulate our *steps of action*. To be as effective as possible, our *vision*, or overriding purpose, must be the bedrock upon which all of our programming is built. *Goals* are the specific, well-defined, and measurable strategic options that enable us to reach the vision we have received. *Action steps* are specific tasks that need to be accomplished to reach our intended goals.

As we look for ways to develop our camping strategy, it is important to keep in mind that every group is different; what may work for one set of kids will bomb with another. That's why it is so important for us to learn how to develop distinct visions and personal strategies. This skill allows us to customize camping ministries to fit individual groups.

Vision

Vision is the ability to see something as it *should* be, in contrast to how it is. An important leadership quality is the foresight to see what needs to be changed and how—I call this vision. A vision, when thought out and defined, becomes the focus of any endeavor.

How do we determine vision? It is easier to do than it sounds, because vision is simply seeing in advance the benefits of any program. For example, the director of a program involving twenty fragmented and disinterested kids should probably have a vision of developing a cohesive and excited group. In this case, the statement of purpose would read, "To build community in such a way that it helps students become excited about their involvement in the Christian faith and in the group."

Take a minute now to determine a mission statement of vision for your event:

1. *Define the current status of your group.* On a sheet of paper, write five statements that describe your group as it is now and estimate for what percentage of your group each statement is true. For example, "very shallow and uncommitted: sixty percent."

2. *Create a scenario.* Write a short paragraph describing the specific progress you want your group to make in the next three years. Take the five statements you made above and divide them into categories, if necessary.

3. *Generate a Mission Statement of Vision.* Using the five status statements and the scenario you just formulated, summarize in one sentence what you want to see happen in your group.

Setting Goals

Our next task is to take that Mission Statement of Vision and decide on specific and measurable targets or *goals*. To be effective, these goals must be chosen with the our kids' needs in mind. We must consciously see the distinction between activities that *we* think would be fun and valuable and those that our *teenagers* would enjoy and, more importantly, would grow through. We must consciously see this distinction if our plans are to meet our kids' needs.

To understand how to develop goals that work toward a chosen Mission Statement of Vision, let's look at one example:

FIRST CHURCH YOUTH GROUP

1. Current Status

Very shallow and uncommitted	(30%)
Attend for social reasons	(30%)
Lonely and outcasts at school	(15%)
Bored with church-related activities	(15%)
Actively desire to follow Christ	(10%)

2. Three-Year Scenario

Our committed kids are student leaders who provide cohesiveness, friendship, and vision to the group as a whole. It is obvious to newcomers that the students involved in the group all have a strong desire for a sense of community. Those who feel lonely or outcast at school know they are valued and loved as members of the community and feel that the youth group is their haven. Even those who attend primarily for social reasons know that, while they are welcome, the commitment of the group as a body is to encourage every person to develop a deeper walk with Jesus Christ. Those who used to be bored now see beyond the "religion" they once disdained and know for themselves how relevant Christ is. The group is also committed to an active faith and care sacrificially for others in need—at home, at school, in the neighborhood, and overseas.

3. Statement of Vision

We at First Church are committed to helping each of our junior and senior high students have a vibrant, committed, and relevant relationship to Jesus Christ, other group members, and our church community; out of these relationships will flow a desire to meet the needs of the world around us.

4. Retreat and Camping Goals

A. In the fall we will have a retreat for the purpose of outreach. Its focus will be on the person of Christ and his relevancy to the students' lives and their world.

B. Out of this retreat will come the formation of small groups for follow-up. The purpose of these groups will be to continue the relationships and the spiritual growth that took place at camp.

C. In early February there will be an intensive retreat focusing on discipleship and commitment to Christ.

D. During spring break we will have a service project that will involve enough travel to instill a sense of youth group community as well as provide an opportunity to serve.

E. During the summer there will be two mini-retreats, both focusing on fellowship, community, and outreach.

F. Also during the summer there will be short-term missions opportunities for students who have been part of a rigorous four-month training program.

Taking Action

Once the vision is drawn and the goals are set, all that remains is to put these goals to work by planning and implementing what I call *action steps*. The best way to ensure that every facet of the retreat is consistent with your vision and goals is to plan *every* conceivable aspect of the retreat far in advance. Although this attention to detail may seem unnecessary, without careful and thorough planning of such mundane things as sleeping arrangements, travel needs, and location, it is easy to end up with a camp that looks "cutting edge" but is really the same dull retreat.

Once your goals are established, those responsible for planning the retreat should meet again, bringing with them only a few tools (such as ideas from this book and others) and a totally blank sheet of paper. In other words, the best way to make sure you are adhering to your vision and goals is to create every camping and retreat experience from the ground up.

A group of youth workers I know in California followed these steps as they planned a week-long summer outreach camp. On the surface, the final schedule didn't look much different from those of previous retreats, but by starting from scratch and taking into account the needs of the students they gave depth to their week that they had never before experienced.

They started with a blank whiteboard and brainstormed what they wanted to accomplish in the lives of kids and leaders during the week. Because they were brainstorming, each idea was given equal weight and none was immediately shot down. After the list was compiled, the group agreed on a few essentials and then moved on to the overall program. They talked about personnel—whether to have a speaker, to have several people do a program, or to have no speaker at all. Next they discussed the schedule and how they could make it reflect their purposes, and finally they tackled the planning of events and competition.

In the end the new camp and the camps of years past looked very similar. The youth workers made only small changes, but those alterations had a tremendous impact on campers' lives. They tried things like ending their competitions one day earlier than usual so the kids would be freed up to relate to one another. On the first night they blindfolded campers as they entered the meeting hall, paired them up with kids from other communities, and had them talk for fifteen minutes—all for the purpose of allowing them to meet others without the stigma of looks. I was the speaker for the week and was asked to get to the focus of my series of messages (the emotional needs of kids) as early as possible, so the kids would feel less inhibited about sharing their hurts, fears, and disappointments.

It was the most powerful camping experience of my life. While we barely scratched the surface of purposeful programming, our bleak effort brought huge rewards. I have never seen young people open up so quickly, and the healing that took place that week was in the realm of the miraculous. I will never go back to "the good old days"! I am sold on creating retreat plans and programs that meet the needs of the students God has given me.

There is no question that it takes far more energy, time, planning, and even prayer to attempt the creation of a unique camp or retreat experience than it does to go by the book. When we make this type of commitment, however, there are several benefits:

- Your team will feel more ownership of the final product.
- Your team will have spent more time together before the Lord.
- You will be forced to work harder at creating a quality experience and will have less of a tendency to wing an event or program.
- Kids will appreciate your efforts to meet current needs, even though most of them will not notice a difference.

As you attempt to personalize your camping strategy, go with your gifts and your heart. Kids change quickly, and groups vary radically in spiritual make up and personality, and only people who know and love their students can design an effective camping program. My purpose in encouraging youth leaders to think strategically is to help them see that this is true. ◆

3

How to Staff and Run Your Camp

I have been able to observe first-hand two philosophical extremes in camp management. On one end of the spectrum is a youth minister who felt the need to run the show. I was to be the camp speaker and we had spent several months talking about how fun camp was going to be and looking forward to spending time talking together about kids and youth ministry. But when I arrived at camp, he was a basket case! Not only was he obviously the only one in charge, he felt the need to have his hand in everything that went on. He was in charge of registering the three groups as they arrived; he led music and accompanied the group on solo guitar. He gave all the announcements, was the late-night disciplinarian, and even counseled a few kids. By the end of the weekend, he could hardly walk!

This past year I also spoke at a camp where the opposite was true. The leadership was so spread out that no one seemed to know what was going on. This retreat was the joint effort of several churches, but every group leader was so careful not to step on anyone else's toes that things got very confusing. Neither the bookkeeper nor registrar, for example, knew who was in charge of paying the bills at the end of the weekend. And there were so many song leaders and announcement givers that the camp never had any continuity up front to draw kids in. As a speaker I had a very difficult time getting the students' attention because I was just one of many faces that paraded across the stage during each general session.

Both of these situations are not just hard on camp leaders; they also affect how kids respond to the Gospel. It really does not matter how large or small a camp, retreat, or conference is—nothing should be left to chance; every detail should be carefully planned. At the same time the responsibility for carrying out those details should be delegated in such a way that the kids sense the leaders' organization and authority; thus, the camp program has continuity.

There are several organizational positions that help to make any size retreat run more smoothly.

Camp Manager

The camp manager is in charge of the entire retreat from the first planning session to its final evaluation. He or she is the one to whom ultimate authority has been given. Camp managers are responsible to see that camps meet their intended purposes and goals. They may have the following responsibilities:

Overseeing the planning process with other staff and all groups attending the camp or conference. They must make sure that opinions are heard and that the philosophy, program, and content of the camp represents the needs of everyone involved. This takes a commitment to communication and thorough pre-event organization, but it will also ensure unity when the camp ends. The camp manager must provide clear directions and expectations for everyone involved. It is the camp manager's responsibility, for example, to let the song leaders know whether they have fifteen or thirty minutes. The more of these decisions that are made in advance, the smoother the camp will run.

Setting a budget, overseeing expenses, and paying bills. It is best to let one person have control of the budget and expenses. Others may be called upon to help with the registration process, but one person should have the final say as to how money is allocated and reimbursed.

Providing spiritual direction and encouragement to the team. So often the planning and running of a camp is treated like some grand task. But more often than not, planning sessions end in hurt feelings, bruised egos, and strained relationships. The camp manager must make sure that the event is more than a task—it should be the creative expression of a group of Christians who love each other and have a common purpose. Every meeting should open with some sort of focus—either a Psalm reading, a short discussion on an article, a quote, or some personal sharing. Anyone committed to producing a camp that will bring glory to Jesus Christ must never see it as purely a task, but as an opportunity to love God and love the body. Besides, when all is said and done, the Holy Spirit is the one responsible for the kids' responses, not those of us "in charge."

Communicating and being a liaison with the property manager. One of my best friends is Bruce Kramer, the property manager for Young Life's oldest and best known camp, Frontier Ranch, in Buena Vista, Colorado (see Bruce's article, "A Word From a Property Manager's Viewpoint," Appendix C). One of the great joys of getting close to Bruce has been having the opportunity to see camping from the "other side." How we treat property staff says a great deal about the sincerity of our faith and mission with kids. They are in Christian camping because they too desire to see Jesus Christ honored and lifted up. They are our partners, not our adversaries. The camp manager should see to it that kids, leaders, and staff members make every person on the property staff feel loved and cared for. Little things like saying thanks for help and asking them how they are doing before we make demands will go a long way toward making property staffers feel valued.

It is also the camp manager's responsibility to make sure that financial expectations are clearly spelled out in writing prior to coming to camp. Some of the ugliest confrontations I have ever seen have occurred when a camp manager and a property manager sat down to finalize the bill!

Being available. Once a retreat begins, the majority of the camp manager's responsibilities will be completed. But in almost every camping situation in which I've had a part, problems and issues have come up that needed immediate attention. Camp managers must be free to make the final calls as these situations arise. This means that unless your retreat is very small, the camp manager should avoid having any added responsibilities during the event.

Being the camp's up-front leader. This is not a necessary responsibility, but it does give the kids a figure head with whom to identify. Whether the up-front leader is the camp manager or someone else, one person should take on the responsibility of being "Mom" or "Dad" of the camp. When the camp manager gives the initial introductions and welcome, explains the rules, and makes all the up-front announcements, it is immediately established that someone is in control.

Program Director(s)

The program director is the person (or persons) in charge of the overall schedule, including the music, games, and any entertainment. Program directors see to it that the program meets the needs of the students; does not overshadow the content or relational emphasis of the camp; does not draw attention to its directors, but instead permits kids to focus on what they are experiencing; enables counselors and campers to build trusting relationships through which the Gospel can best be heard; and provides an atmosphere that enables students to be themselves.

This is a tall order, but when someone is given specific responsibility for the program, he or she can focus on these issues without being sidetracked. Although program directors are often chosen for their ability to be humorous in front of a crowd, they must also be extremely organized and able to delegate. Even the smallest camps take well-oiled schedules to ensure that kids have the best weekend of their lives.

Program directors may have the following responsibilities:

Planning and developing a program that reflects the Gospel. Program directors are responsible for making sure that every student feels loved and special. While laughter is an important element in an enjoyable program, issues of competition, community, and self-esteem touch kids more deeply. Program directors must pray through every aspect of the camp to gain sensitivity and to love kids just as they are.

Setting the program budget under the direction of the camp manager. The program director must see to it that receipts are kept and careful records are made of all expenses. The camp manager should reimburse for these shortly after the event.

Overseeing all up-front personnel except camp manager and speaker. The program director must ensure that everything happening up front is consistent with the camp's purposes. Every announcement (other than those given by the camp manager), every song, and every skit must be reviewed and discussed with the program director before its presentation. It is the program director's responsibility to see that everyone involved in the camp program is well prepared and has the camp's purpose clearly in mind.

Organizing all activities. The program director's job includes developing and implementing games, competitions, and mixers so that they are as enjoyable as possible. The only way to do this is to plan thoroughly and communicate clearly to all involved the purpose and rules for each activity. For example, as creative and sophisticated as some of today's camp games are, many fail for two reasons: either the support personnel has no idea how to make the game run smoothly, or the game leader does a poor job of explaining the game. In a well-planned program, each game is clearly described on a sheet of paper and these directions are handed out in advance to any personnel involved in running the game.

Head Counselors

Almost every retreat or camp needs someone to be in charge of security and discipline. But the task of the head counselor is much more than that. Head counselors really have two roles. First, they are responsible for any discipline and security issues; and second, they are ministers to those who are in the cabins with kids and the camp's counselors.

Specifically, head counselors have the following responsibilities:

Ensuring that campers behave according to the rules of the camp. Some groups have called these the *Camp Cops*, others simply *Security*, and others *Deans*. The choice of the term *Head Counselor* is better suited because the position should be more relational than confrontational. The majority of our students do not need more authorities in their lives; they need friends. When we do need to implement tough love, we should *always* do so within the context of a loving relationship. When inappropriate behavior is observed, they should treat the offending young people with respect, tenderness, and great care. For example, head counselors should avoid yelling from a distance at students to obey the rules.

Head counselors should be the last to go to bed at night and should do so only after they have ensured that all of the students are in their cabins for the evening. (Once the students are in their cabins for the night, the head counselor is no longer responsible for them. It is the counselor's responsibility to make sure that no raids take place and that the campers all stay in their cabins until morning.)

There are times, however, when students need strict discipline, and in these situations the head counselor should work with that student's counselor (and, if appropriate, the leader of the student's youth group) to determine the needed disciplinary action. If misconduct is severe, the camp manager should be called on to make the final decision about expulsion from the camp. In such cases, the head counselor should not make any threats or decisions without pulling other leaders in for counsel. As we follow the biblical mandate (Matthew 18) to come together in agreement with two or three members of the body before confronting a wrongdoing, we can avoid misunderstandings.

Leading the counseling staff. Because this is a ministry position and not simply a security force, head counselors are in an ideal position to advise and minister to those who counsel kids. To refresh the counselors in the midst of the battle, there should be daily (at least) counselor meetings to provide opportunities for worship, sharing, prayer, quiet, and training.

Head counselors should aim to informally advise and guide counselors in their dealings with kids. They should be at all events and meetings, observing the counselors' interactions with their students and should also be available to help counselors who are in situations over their heads. To accomplish this, head counselors must seek to build one-on-one relationships with as many counselors as possible.

Work-Crew/Work-Staff Boss

Very few of the camps I have attended have had a vision for using work crews to serve the campers, but work crews are a great ministry opportunity. A work crew usually is comprised of two kinds of students: those who have been to camp before and are ready for a different kind of challenge, and those who are in the twilight-zone period of life in which they are no longer kids but are not quite ready to be counselors. Work crews involve these kids in the action of the camp and allow them to learn the importance of serving others at the same time.

The ratio of work-crew members to campers should be about one to ten; if there are fifty campers, for example, you should have a work crew of five. If the camp leaders choose to charge the work crew participants full camp tuition, it is best to either offer large scholarships to crew members or give them enough time off so that they can enjoy the camp. On the other hand, once a camp's managers are made aware of the purpose of the work crew, the fee usually can be significantly reduced. A Young Life property like Frontier Ranch, for example, generally just charges work-crew students for their meals and even houses them in specially reserved cabins.

The work crew has the following responsibilities:

Serving as waiters and waitresses. This means that the work crew will have to eat before or after the campers and should treat the campers as if they were in a restaurant. After the meal is over, the work crew is also responsible for cleaning up.

When not serving meals, the work crew helps with the program in any way necessary. Work-crew members can fill up water balloons, set cones out on the field, or hang curtains to create a stage for the entertainment. The work crew can also provide the program planners with enough hands to pull off quality events and leave the counselors more time to build relationships with their students. Because time on a weekend retreat is limited, it is especially important for the work crew to be available to help with the program so that things can run as efficiently as possible.

Work-crew bosses have the responsibility of overseeing work crews. Their task is two-fold: first of all, bosses work alongside crew members to ensure that their service and attitudes reflect the objectives of the camp. As work-crew bosses work alongside their crew members, they are able to model a servant's attitude and also keep a close eye on how the crew is doing. A work-crew boss is essential to ensure that the work crew does a top-notch job.

Second, the work-crew boss acts as the work crew's minister. There should be some work-crew meetings in which members focus their thoughts on Christ and Scripture, on sharing, and on praying for the camp—both its leaders and campers. The work-crew boss should also see these times as opportunities to counsel work-crew kids, to build relationships with them, and to challenge them in their personal walks with Christ. If possible, try to arrange the work crew's schedule so that its members can hear as many messages as possible.

Counselor

The counselor is the heart of a relational Christian camping experience. The entire program and message should be designed to enable counselors to build relationships with campers, so that every young person has an adult who can help him or her sort out the meaning of the Gospel personally.

The counselor-to-camper ratio should be no more than one to ten; the ideal is one counselor for every five to seven students. If at all possible, a counselor should have no responsibilities other than caring for the students in his or her cabin. Almost every camp violates this philosophy and the campers suffer for it. Even if it costs a little more money, most of the responsibilities for running the camp should be handled by people who are *not* in the cabins with kids. As everyone else on the camp staff does his or her job, the counselors can be totally freed up to care for each kid in their cabins. This is the ultimate purpose for having a camp staff—so that the counselors have every opportunity to spend time with their kids.

Counselors have the following responsibilities:

Building trust relationships with every camper in their cabins. This may be obvious to some, but more often than not Christian camping counselors see themselves more as chaperons than as friends. A chaperon, for example, would feel free to stand in the back during a meeting or sit back drinking a cup of coffee during a skit presented during a meal. A friend who is intent on building a trusting relationship with a kid, on the other hand, is far more likely to be the first to set down the coffee mug and enthusiastically applaud a skit's presentation. Counselors who really love their kids will sit with them at every meeting (as near the front as possible!), sing loudly right along with them, give them a "high-five" after a fun skit, and relax with them during free time. Connecting with kids is a counselor's greatest joy, and everyone who counsels must be committed to building solid relationships.

Interpreting the Gospel for their campers. As gifted as a speaker may be, there is no way that one person can know enough about every student in a camp to make the Gospel come alive for each of them. The job of the counselor is to use the relationships they have built with their students as bridges between the speaker and young people. This should happen both formally and informally over the course of a camp.

Formally, the program should have built-in opportunities for students to interact with the content of the message in the cabin setting. Often called *cabin time*, these meetings allow the counselor to find out what the kids heard (get them talking) and make sure that the content of the message was clear. If, after all the students have shared in a cabin time, counselors realize that their campers have missed some key points the speaker was trying to make, they should give *short* explanations of those points. At all costs, however, counselors should not use cabin time to give kids another message! To use finesse in leading a cabin time, we must balance on the fine line of allowing campers to say what they think, and make sure that they heard what the speaker was trying to communicate. This takes training as well as practice, and inexperienced counselors should always have the opportunity to be assistants to experienced counselors.

Informally, counselors should seek to discuss the content of messages one-on-one with every student in their cabins before they go home. A good counselor will always make an effort to relate individually with kids. The best way to follow up in a one-on-one situation is to discuss each student's statements during the last cabin time. Some of the best counselors I know will make fifteen-minute appointments with kids for either the last day of camp or for the bus ride home.

Following up every student. We have trained our counselors to try to meet with every student individually within two weeks of returning from camp, if at all possible. These meetings are useful to ensure that the students have been able to take what they learned and decided while at camp back into the "real world." Some leaders have used the camp and cabin times to begin small-group Bible studies or discussion groups. Follow ups are essential if students are to apply what they learned at camp, and counselors are the only people with both the commitment and the relationships to make those follow ups meaningful.

For a camp to run smoothly, responsibilities should be divided among enough people to carry the load, but not so many that no one knows who is in charge of what. The essential positions have been mentioned in this chapter: camp manager, program director, head counselor, work-crew boss and work crews, and counselors. For different camps, retreats, and conferences, there may be a few other positions of responsibility that will need to be structured, but for almost every camp or conference setting, the ones I've listed are essential.

The important thing to remember is that for a camp to fulfill its purposes, every student must have the individual and relational touch of an adult who cares for him or her, and this person needs to be freed up to simply be with kids. The more we do to facilitate the relationships of counselors to campers, the better the chances that we will pull off a great retreat. ◆

4

◆ ◆ ◆

Vital Ingredients for a Successful Camp

What separates an outstanding retreat or camp from one best described as mediocre? I can't remember the last camp I attended where everyone involved felt like we "hit the long ball." Usually there has been some glaring flaw or deficiency that has made the evaluation slightly uncomfortable. Either the skits were inappropriate, the budget was too lean (or too fat!), or insurance needs were overlooked. Maybe the food was bad, or kids were out of control, or the games were disorganized. Seldom did everything fall into place just right.

I don't guarantee a perfect camping experience to those who follow this book exactly, but I have tried to think through as many angles as possible to give a prepared team the best shot at a quality experience. There are chapters on volunteers, music, humor, and camp staffing. But many general issues don't fall into any one category and yet are fundamental to any camp's success. Here are some of the vital ingredients needed to make a camp or retreat a winner.

Schedule

Most of the camps and conferences I attend give campers a schedule upon their arrival. This is a mistake: First, it allows kids to decide beforehand what they are not going to like. Whether it is an event or a speaker, students who make up their mind about something, even in ignorance, are hard to win back. Second, all of us like to be surprised, and if students are a part of an unfolding camping experience, they tend to be more excited.

You can tell students the things they really *need* to know from meal to meal or meeting to meeting, but don't let on to the schedule more than a day at a time. Give all of the announcements at the end of each meal so students will not be tempted to leave early. This allows counselors to enjoy a relaxed, nonpressured meal, knowing that they will always have a few minutes to talk with kids around the table before they rush off. Even counselors don't really need a schedule beforehand (although they may *think* they do); they can be told things a day ahead of the kids at the counselor meeting.

Budgets and Finances

One of the biggest headaches of putting together retreats of any size is trying to come up with a workable budget that fulfills the goals of the event without destroying the youth budget. Unless you were an accounting major at school, camp finances may be a legitimate fear. With advance planning and a little homework, however, you can avoid those "final bill blues."

All camps and retreats have fixed costs: transportation, meals and lodging, and insurance, to name a few. There are many other expenses, however, over which we *do* have control: costs for speakers, musicians, T-shirts, mailings, and so on. The farther in advance we can determine our fixed costs, the more flexible we can be with "other" items. Many camp planners work backwards (hire a speaker and musician first) and end up losing a lot of money.

If you have done your homework and know that you expect, for example, two hundred students at your camp, and that each will contribute ten dollars toward hiring a speaker and a musician, you are now in a position to negotiate. For example, when you call a speaker, you can explain the retreat and let the person know immediately what you can reasonably afford. During the conversation it is a good idea to ask speakers what they usually receive, for they use different methods for coming up with a fee. And not all speakers are in a position to negotiate, so you may have to either offer more or find someone else.

On the other hand, some will tell you their fee but accept what you can afford. From a speaker's point of view, I greatly appreciate it when a host is honest and forthright.

For many musicians, the process is a little different. Agents usually do the booking (if they don't go through an agent, treat them as you would a speaker). An agent may or may not be flexible with the artist's fee, depending on a variety of factors. Again, the best policy is to be candid about your needs and budget and see what happens. (Whenever you book an artist for any camp or retreat, insist on talking directly to him or her prior to the event. Too many musicians have completely missed a crowd because they didn't understand what the students needed.)

Years ago my first boss in youth ministry taught me how to go to camp without ever losing money. For the most part, as I've followed his instructions I have had great success. (I've been in Young Life most of my career, and when we lose money at camp, it affects our paychecks, so we learn quickly!) The secret to his strategy is planning the budget on a "per camper" basis, as opposed to basing it on overall expenses. Here's an example:

FRONTIER RANCH WEEKEND CAMP
Sample Budget[1]

1. Fixed costs:

Housing/meals	37.00 (per person)
Transportation[2]	20.00
T-shirts	4.10 (per student; leaders optional)
Total fixed cost:	$61.10 (per person)

2. Program expenses (divided by 90)

Speaker (Trans. only)	2.35	(Flight = $210.00)
Program	3.65	(Misc. needs = $300.00)
Total program	$6.00	

3. Base expense $67.10

---

1 For ninety kids and fifteen leaders.
2 Based on per-bus cost of $600 round trip at 30 campers per bus.

4. **Cost per student to help with scholarships, sign-up shortages, etc.** $7.90

5. **Cost per camper** $75.00

   Cost per counselor $37.00

Permission Slips and Insurance

In the modern world of litigation it is hard to imagine that there is a need to discuss this, but in case there remains some confusion in this area, here is a sample Parental Consent Form that can be used for almost any situation.

PARENTAL CONSENT FOR MEDICAL TREATMENT

[   ] always carries accident insurance for participants in any [   ] activity. Your son or daughter is planning to participate in one of these activities.

With the increasing sophistication of our medical systems, we are finding it expedient to have parental release forms in the unlikely event of some serious injury requiring medical treatment.

This release gives us permission to take your child to the nearest available medical facility and have the necessary treatment administered. This is not necessary from our perspective, but from your perspective, as many hospitals will not administer any medical atention to a minor without some parental consent.

Therefore, would you please read the statement in capital letters and add your signature to it. All this does is give us the permission to seek whatever medical attention we deem necessary. Our insurance is explained below.

IN CASE OF EMERGENCY, I UNDERSTAND THAT EVERY EFFORT WILL BE MADE TO CONTACT ME. IF I CANNOT BE REACHED, I HEREBY GIVE [   ] THE PERMISSION TO ACT IN MY BEHALF IN SEEKING EMERGENCY TREATMENT FOR MY CHILD IN THE EVENT THAT SUCH TREATMENT IS DEEMED NECESSARY BY [   ]. I GIVE

PERMISSION TO THOSE ADMINISTERING EMERGENCY TREATMENT TO DO SO, USING THOSE MEASURES DEEMED NECESSARY. I ABSOLVE [   ] FROM LIABILITY IN ACTING ON MY BEHALF IN THIS REGARD SO LONG AS [   ] IS NOT GROSSLY NEGLIGENT.

_____

Name of child (please print)

_____

Signature of parent or guardian   Phone

If parents are not available, please call relative below:

_____

Name   Phone

_____

Street Address   City & State   Zip

Additional comments regarding medical history, allergies, penicillin or drug reactions, etc., which may be needed in any treatment:

_____

_____

_____

There is no deductible with the [   ] coverage. The first $250 in medical expense is covered by the [   ] insurance entirely. Any amount incurred above that will be coordinated with your personal insurance. At that point, the [   ] insurance will become the secondary carrier and will supplement your coverage. The maximum amount available from the [   ] insurance is [$].[3]

Parent or guardian's insurance company _____

Address of parent or guardian's insurance company

_____

Policy number of parent or guardian's insurance _____

_____

[3] You will need to replace this paragraph with the specific terms of your insurance policy.

Even when using a form like this, every youth worker should contact a friendly local attorney for advice as to local and state laws. Whenever we transport young people, certain laws and insurance regulations must be taken seriously. Most insurance companies require that those driving kids to a camp (or to any event) be over twenty-one years of age and strongly recommend that they complete a driver safety course. Many hospitals will admit only those with very serious injuries without parental consent.

Competition

Tony Campolo, in his book *Growing Up in America* (Grand Rapids: YS/Zondervan, 1989), states: "The competitive lifestyle engendered by American society creates tremendous fear and self-doubt in the psyche of young people." Given my experience in Christian camping, I tend to agree with him. Not only are winners more excited and involved, losers seem more apt to lose interest altogether. Campolo's solution—to eliminate competition altogether—is one solution.

Another solution, however, is to get more creative with our competitive events. The best camp game I have ever seen maintained a sense of competition but only enough to motivate the campers to give it their best shot. The game was actually a giant relay race, and each team (the camp was broken up into four teams) was split into two teams (i.e., Miners A and B team), so there were eight groups competing. Each team began the race at a station where they would spend three minutes (a shotgun told them when to move to the next station) trying to perform a competitive task (win a trivia contest, pull a raft holding two team members across a swimming pool, put in free throws, shoot a frisbee golf course, etc.). When the relay was over, everyone was thoroughly exhausted but overwhelmingly elated. And because the event was a relay, its competitive element was almost forgotten.

If you plan on holding competitive events, you can defuse their intensity by avoiding the announcement of results until the "Awards Ceremony" near the end of the event. Kids will accept this practice, especially if their counselors are behind it. During the awards ceremony, you might just announce first place—and keep even this announcement low key; but be sure to give some individual awards to kids, or even cabin groups, who could use some encouragement. One group combined an awards dinner with a lip-sync contest in an attempt to make the event fun for everyone.

Games and Activities

Games and mixers are perhaps as central to the smooth running of a camp as any other event. When we gather students for an overnight experience, whether we have ten or five thousand, their primary desire is to have fun and ours is to give them a meaningful experience. Games meet both desires—campers enjoy themselves and at the same time develop relationships and a sense of community that will allow them to drop the façades that hinder the gospel. Games must be properly planned and organized to accomplish these goals.

But running a quality game is harder than it sounds. The process is the same for any game, regardless of the camp's size: Get the crowd's attention by blowing a whistle and have the counselors clued in that they are to get the troops quiet (this grass-roots help is a *must!*). Next, briefly explain the point of the game and give a very quick demonstration, if necessary. (When everyone understands what is going on, they can do a better job of participating.) Keep the instructions and preparation fast-moving; it is very difficult to keep an entire camp's attention during dead time, especially outdoors. Once the game begins, play fun, upbeat background music to increase the group's excitement level (e.g., Beach Boys, marches, fast country, Amy Grant, Petra).

Three different types of activities are most often used in a camp setting: *Mixers*, *Olympics*, and *Big Events*.

Mixers. These games break down social barriers and help campers get acquainted. By definition they must involve every person and must mix the crowd so that strangers are thrown together.

Here is an example of an excellent camp mixer:

- **Anatomy Groupers.** When the music (either live guitar or taped) starts, have every person in camp, including counselors, begin mingling, moving in and out around each other, and basically toward the room's center. When the music stops and a whistle is blown, everyone freezes. The leader then shouts out the name of a body part ("Ear!"), a number ("Three!"), and "GO!" At that point players get into groups of three with their ears touching. After two or three practice rounds, judges begin dismissing those who are not in groups within five seconds (or so). In order to keep interest up, eliminate players slowly at first and then quickly reduce the group's size until a final remaining few can be declared winners.

Olympics. These are usually competitive games or relays (see *Competition* above) that have a teamwork emphasis. Olympics are good tools with which to bring different groups of kids together; with good counselor modeling, students can build relationships as they root for their team's success.

In the best Olympics I have seen the counselors acted as officials, coaches, and photographers, but not as participants (except in whole-team events, such as a "Goldfish Grab" in the swimming pool). The counselors' role in an Olympics is to ensure that all the kids in their cabin are participating and enjoying the event. Many times guys are paired up with girls, for example, and the counselors should help pair kids in such a way that they all feel included and liked.

The Big Event. This term is most often used to describe the game held on Saturday afternoon at a weekend camp. Whether it is a huge mudfight vaguely disguised as "Capture the Flag" or some other game, an all-camp function on a Saturday afternoon brings a camp together. It is very important to inform counselors that this is not an optional event; they must be involved. The point of this type of game is to build trust and community and this is crucial to the development of counselor/counselee relationships. Once kids know you love them enough to let them throw you in the mud, you have a friend for life!

Meals

Mealtimes will provide one of your best counseling opportunities. For forty-five minutes three times a day, the program is committed to nothing but building relationships. But there are some things that should be considered if you are to make the most of the time.

- Counselors should enter the dining hall at least five minutes before the campers are admitted and make sure that each table has at least one counselor.
- Campers should be let in all at once. This will enable the camp manager, program directors, and head counselors to communicate with the counselors. And if the kids enter the dining hall as a unit while fun music plays, in

the scramble they will often mingle more freely than if they are allowed to saunter in.

- When you rent a property, usually you do have some say in the menu. It is a good idea to at least ask for options—poor camp food is as much our problem as the camp manager's.

- If you have a work crew, don't let kids (or leaders!) walk around during meals—this makes their job more difficult.

- Except during specific program times, avoid cheering and chanting in the dining hall. Things like "This is table number one, where is number two?" do nothing to enhance relationships or the atmosphere. Help students behave in the dining hall as they would in a restaurant.

Rules

One of the first things done in every camp or retreat is rule-reading. Most of the time a counselor or member of the property staff will stand up at the first meal and tell the students all the things they are not allowed to do. The message kids often come away with is akin to "Thou shalt not have fun!" And then the head of security goes into the penalties for missing meetings or meals, guys being in girls' cabins, and general horsing around. Before the event has even begun, we remind kids that they are untrustworthy and are being watched.

Some groups have gotten more creative in the way they present rules. One group prints them in an information manual that every student receives on arrival. The manual seems less negative because rules are listed as expectations and are intermingled with other necessary information. Another group emphasizes that the camp is a family or *township*, calls rules "strong suggestions," and uses humor to share a limited number of rules without mentioning the severity of their consequences. One church group I know makes their expectations clear on the brochure and doesn't list the rules at camp at all! Whatever you choose to do, remember that rules can immediately set a negative tone, so be as creative as you can when you tell them to the kids.

Setting parameters is essential; without them a retreat can quickly fall apart. Usually the hardest infractions to discuss are those that have the greatest potential to harm relationships, like cabin raiding (raids can really sour property staff and even injure kids). Here is a list of some recommended essential rules for a Christian youth retreat:

1. Smoke only in designated areas.
2. Once the cabin bell (or its equivalent) sounds, no one is allowed outside his or her cabin except in emergencies. (This is important for several reasons: to avoid raids, to give the head counselors a chance to sleep, and to have some way of knowing were everyone is.)
3. Guys and girls should remain in their own cabin areas and should never be in each other's rooms. (This helps the counselors make rooms available for honest relationship building and discourages the temptation for sexual involvement or at least makes it a lot less convenient!)
4. Everyone is expected to attend every function, including all meals (the schedule and announcements are given there), meetings, and events. (If a student is sick, the counselor should notify the nurse or doctor and the student's absence is excusable.) ◆

◆ ◆ ◆

5

Volunteers: Mining Your Hidden Treasure

My best high-school camp memory is of being in the cabin with my favorite leader, Bruce. He was huge and had a big bushy beard and clothes that looked slept in. He owned a construction firm, and I can't remember ever seeing him clean. But Bruce loved me, and that was all that mattered!

That weekend was my first exposure to a youth retreat, and was it a wild one! We played a game on Saturday afternoon called Wells Fargo, in which two teams of three hundred kids tried to rip a piece of tape off the foreheads of their opponents. We were the "Cowboys," so we had yellow tape, and as soon as the gun went off ten "Indians" with red tape came after our little group. "Stay with me!" Bruce yelled. "I'll take care of you guys." And while five of us sophomore guys looked on, he did!

Bruce, a six-foot, two-inch, 240-pound, thirty-five-year-old contractor, just stood there as these guys ran forward. They seemed pretty formidable (all football stars from a rival high school), and they were out to clobber us! As soon as they got within five feet of Bruce, he let out a yell and nailed the first kid—in one hit! It was incredible. To this day I haven't forgotten how our jaws dropped watching our spiritual leader be so out of control.

Bruce had a great heart, and we loved him, but I can imagine the headache he must have been to other staff members. He was hard to lead because he was so committed to his ministry that he fought to get the most and best for "his kids." He rarely attended meetings, usually because he felt that he didn't have the time and that they weren't really necessary for someone with his focus, commitment, and experience. He was called to work with kids, and that's what he did.

Next to the Holy Spirit and the Bible, volunteers are the most valuable resource churches have. Volunteers cannot be categorized, for they are all unique and bring specialized gifts to a ministry team. It is a common mistake in churches and youth ministry programs to view volunteer staff as helpers or as tools in the hands of the paid staff. Every effective program that I have seen relies heavily on the commitment, wisdom, and talent of volunteers. Usually they are the ones directly involved with the students as counselors or leaders, but successful programs also utilize those adults who want to serve but aren't all that effective with kids. Veteran youth-worker Jim Burns states, "The quality and quantity of any youth ministry program directly depends on the adult involvement in the program" (*The Youth Builder*, Eugene: Harvest House, 1988).

What a gift a team of dedicated volunteers is! They are wonderful because they are willing to make incredible sacrifices to help kids. But to free them up to minister effectively, those of us in leadership must make sure we understand what makes volunteers "tick." Bruce, for example, was invaluable as a leader, but he often got into trouble because he wasn't a "team player." His indepedence left him on his own for training, accountability, and support, and this in turn caused him to sometimes do or say things that later came back to hurt him and his ministry. Leaders, even volunteer ones, must see that nurturing volunteer staff is as important to youth ministry as working directly with youth.

Portrait of a Volunteer

A volunteer is anyone who commits to active participation in a program they feel is important. While most youth workers, professional or volunteer, are emotionally and spiritually healthy adults who love kids and want to serve them in the name of Christ, there are those who have mixed motives for working with young people. For example, some leaders may be involved with a program because it makes them feel good or because they enjoy the *tasks* of the ministry (teaching Sunday school, for example) and not because they genuinely love kids. Or their motivation may spring from a need to relieve a sense of guilt, from some need for attention or affirmation, or from any combination of reasons.

When a paid youth worker displays any of these motivations, church leaders normally take steps to see that the individual moves on. But because many programs are in such desperate need of volunteer staff, these weaknesses or wrong motives are often overlooked or ignored. This is a dangerous tendency. Both professionals and volunteers need to have integrity, honesty, and spiritual and psychological health. Young people need models they can follow, people who follow Christ in such a way that their motives are beyond question. Always take the time to carry out stringent interviews and then help your chosen counselors develop habits of mutual accountability. Too often we grab counselors at the last minute to fill a need, and stories abound of groups that deeply regret their laxness.

Some volunteers, especially newcomers, secretly wonder about their effectiveness and value in the program and feel that their lack of time or personal inadequacies will make them useless. And many times volunteers are frustrated and sometimes even bitter because they are not allowed to give input. When one or more of these issues gets discouraging enough, even the most loyal volunteers can become disillusioned and fade away. They burn out on the work they once loved and often wait years before returning to any volunteer service. In most youth programs, as paid staffers come and go, dedicated volunteer adults keep things together. They deserve our friendship, time, prayer, and efforts because they are the heart and hands of the body of Christ.

What a Volunteer Needs From Leadership

How can we give a caring response to the makeup and needs of volunteers? How can we encourage volunteers and establish in them a sense of group ownership? How can we best avoid burnout, bitterness, and frustration? For volunteers to be healthy and excited throughout their ministry, I believe they need *training and nurturing*, a sense of *ownership*, and clear *job expectations*.

Training and nurturing. Bruce was a classic case of how an initial lack of training evolved into a disdain for instruction. He made many blunders and lacked some leadership skills necessary in high-school ministries. Early on, he may have welcomed help, but as he gained confidence in his gifts and became established in his position, he closed himself to all input. Bruce would have been better equipped, healthier, and even enjoyed himself more if he had been trained from the outset of his ministry and had been encouraged (and expected) to continue being trained throughout his volunteer stint.

Training is essentially the enabling of a person to perform a given function. It involves four steps: *initiation, on-the-job practice, evaluation,* and *advanced and/or specialized training.*

- **Initiation.** In camp counseling, initiation involves taking every *direct-ministry volunteer* (those who have any direct contact with campers) through a comprehensive training course. As I researched this book, I was unable to find a single resource published to meet this need. Because of this, I've included Appendix A, an excerpt from *A Resource Guide for Camp Counselors,* compiled by Stan Beard, director of ministry resources for Young Life, and have used it with the permission of Young Life, Inc. While this resource must be modified to fit your particular camp, it will provide a starting point from which to begin creating your volunteer training course.

- **On-the-job practice.** No first-time counselor should be expected to go through a counselor training course and then immediately handle a cabin of kids solo. Training must be on-the-job, and every direct-ministry volunteer (and even staff person!) should be given the chance to be a junior counselor with an experienced leader on their first go-round. As the week or weekend progresses, junior counselors should be given opportunities to lead cabin times, games, and activities, and should initiate some one-on-one times with selected campers.

- **Evaluation.** The third phase of training is evaluation. New counselors should not be given responsibilities without careful observation and evaluation. After junior counselors finish leading cabin times, for example, their senior counselors should sit down with them and give them a thorough evaluation. For these evaluations to be helpful, senior leaders should be specific. Instead of saying, "Great job, Sue!", they should try saying things like, "I appreciated the way you grabbed the students' attention, had everyone share without making them feel embarrassed, and kept the discussion going." Even more productive is for the trainer to come up with a list of three or four areas needing improvement as well as three or four specific positives deserving praise. For example, "I noticed that Jill seemed to want to dominate; it may be helpful to call on some of the quieter kids before she gets a chance to say so much." With this type of guidance, an inexperienced counselor can quickly pick up what it takes to be an effective camp counselor.

- **Advanced and/or specialized training.** As volunteers become more capable and confident, continue to train, stretch, and lead them. Offer courses and resource opportunities for experienced counselors that deal with hurting kids, recognizing and identifying painful issues, and advanced listening skills to help sharpen your seasoned volunteers as they become more integral to your youth ministry program. Companies such as Youth Specialties offer books, periodicals, and seminars for use in training experienced volunteers. We need to remember that it is important never to let even our best and most experienced volunteers or staff get to the point of feeling they know all there is to know about working effectively with adolescents.

Ownership. As volunteers are trained in ministry tasks, they will begin to develop ideas and opinions about how best to run a program. They will sometimes be able to spot weaknesses that we professionals miss or choose to overlook. This is one of the greatest gifts that volunteers bring to an organization—and once trained they often offer more to the ministry than its paid staff.

Most seasoned youth workers would at least nod their assent to my theories about the value of volunteers. But in practice, most leaders demonstrate just the opposite: volunteer camp counselors are treated like raw recruits who have neither the experience nor the training to warrant a voice in what goes on in a camping program. They can counsel, cook, drive, and raise money, but they are given no input on decisions like budgets, content, schedule, and the speaker or musician choice, as if such matters were out of their range of expertise.

There is an axiom of youth ministry that states: the more input people have, the deeper their commitments and loyalties will be. This axiom certainly holds in camping ministries. Once we teach our volunteers the basics of Christian youth camping, we must allow our senior direct-ministry volunteers to develop a sense of ownership. For the sake of the program as well as their continued commitment and involvement, we must applaud and encourage their insights, relational skills, business savvy, life experience, and wisdom.

I first met Tim Personius when we were trying to recruit adult volunteers for an outreach ministry in a local high school. I was immediately attracted to his warm and outgoing personality. When we met to discuss his involvement, his response was open but hesitant. He struggled with questions of insecurity. "Do I have the time? Will I be any good? Will kids respond to me? Do I like kids enough to give myself away to them?" These questions and others forced Tim to take time praying and considering how significant a commitment he was willing to make.

Tim did decide to get involved, and as we continued to meet I began to realize that for Tim to step into the senior leadership of Miraleste High School's outreach club, he would have to know that he was in charge—that's the kind of guy he was, a natural leader. As I assured him that he would be responsible for ministering to both kids and leaders, he rose to the occasion and built one of the best ministries I have ever seen. He and his team of volunteers very quickly developed a tremendous program—creative, relational, attractive, and extremely effective.

Within a year Tim and I were meeting as friends, co-laborers, and ministry peers, even though I was full time in the ministry and he was full time in marketing. He cared every bit as much as I did about our program and where we were headed and constantly reminded me that he had just as much invested in the ministry as I had. Tim's sense of ownership was one of the greatest and most valued gifts during my years in Southern California—I had a friend and a partner, someone on whom I could lean and with whom I could walk.

There are several ways to foster ownership in volunteers. The simplest is for staffers in charge of given camps or retreats to make pacts with their adult-ministry teams and assure them that they will be involved, at least at a committee level, in every major decision as the camp is planned and executed. As this invitation is extended, volunteers will feel more freedom to give input. Another way is to habitually take on partners who will walk through every responsibility and decision with you as you run a camp. These folks may not be as experienced as you are, but as they are included in leadership decisions, they will respond with care and responsibility.

Instilling ownership may be as simple as giving volunteers freedom to speak their minds. Often what bars volunteers from feeling a sense of ownership and value is an unspoken feeling that what they think doesn't matter. Wise youth workers responsible for a group of volunteers will speak often and loudly about everyone's importance and the fact that it takes a team to run a program effectively.

Job expectations. There are two main areas of involvement for volunteers in a camping program—service and support, and direct-ministry or counseling opportunities. Adults who would like simply to "help out" are often best plugged in to specific assignments. This accomplishes several things:

- The more adults we involve in our programs the greater the number of people we will have committed to it. The most effective youth ministries have a wide range of adults involved at every level. And once someone is exposed to our programs and has a positive experience, even on a limited, task-only basis, they often want to get more deeply involved.

- Not everyone has the time or ability to work directly with young people, but they still may sense a call to love kids and have an impact on their lives. As leaders of youth programs, we need to do all we can to provide ministry opportunities for them.

- So many details contribute to an effective and well-run camping experience that the more help we have, the better. While it is true that having a greater number of volunteers makes coordination and initial effort more necessary, the greater number of hands will also provide a much greater resource pool in the long run.

- When problems or issues affect the youth program, it never hurts to have a large number of adults involved who know both the staff and the kids. Church or board politics sometimes force youth-ministry programs to call on lay people who have had first-hand experience to speak out on the ministry's behalf. Many times those adults with whom we have worked will be the program's most ardent supporters.

VOLUNTEER SERVICE AND SUPPORT TASKS

Drivers

Cooks

Work Crew (see chapter 3)

Calling Committee: for communications prior to and following the camp.

Prayer Chain

Speaker/Musician Liaison: to take care of arrangements, contracts, payment, travel, and other miscellaneous needs.

Program Gofer: to be available to help out with logistics.

Medical Assistance: to care for minor illnesses or injuries or to be a resource for dealing with more serious problems. (This is a great way to expose doctors or nurses to the program.)

Counselor: to advise counselors. Because we are dealing with so many "at risk" kids, having a trained, licensed counselor available is a tremendous tool.

Photographer: to make still, slide, and video recordings of the camp's activities. These are important when you need to show others what happened at camp, when you want to publicize your youth ministry, and when you and your group just want to reminisce.

Board Member: to report on the youth program and become familiar with its activities.

Final Notes on Direct Ministry

Volunteers involved in direct ministry usually take on the role of counselor for a camp or retreat. As mentioned earlier in this chapter, the more well-trained and experienced direct-ministry adults are, the more effective a program will be; that is the key. We must give classroom *and* on-the-job training before we place anyone in a position to lead kids; their role is too critical.

The tasks of a counselor are vast and situational—they are the personal link between the camp staff and the campers. They share cabins with their students (they should never have their own rooms), make sure their kids are enjoying themselves and feeling included, and should be available to spend time with individuals. But, in the final analysis, the only way to become an effective counselor is through experience and constructive evaluation. ◆

6

♦ ♦ ♦

How to Use Music and Singing

Mount Herman Christian Conference Center, in the foothills of Santa Cruz, California, was where it started for me. I'll never forget sitting with my high-school buddies and going absolutely crazy over the imitation Beach-Boys band that was the closing skit of Saturday night's entertainment. It was fun, wild, exciting, and—surprisingly—quality. We were overwhelmed with the amount of work and effort that had gone into a simple night of skits. That commitment to give campers the very best has stuck with me ever since. The night held a double bonus really, because I saw how music, which I loved, could be used to bring kids to Christ, albeit in a round about way!

Because music is so universal and powerful, and because it has the ability to deeply touch souls, it is one of our most important tools in youth ministry. From its ability to create a sense of worship, awe, and wonder, to the way it can set a tone for adventure and excitement, music can greatly enhance our efforts to reach kids. But, like any other powerful instrument, music can also be a negative and even destructive force when used casually or thoughtlessly. This chapter focuses on the great gift of music—its use and misuse—and gives some tips on using music effectively to reach kids.

Group Singing

When I have the opportunity to speak at a young people's camp or conference, the single biggest advantage the schedule planners can give me is a focused and well-prepared audience. By far the best way to accomplish this is to have some group singing just prior to the message. Many groups ignore this means of building community and focus. As a result, even when singing is part of the schedule, often fifteen minutes of announcements is sandwiched between the singing and the message. This completely destroys whatever sense of community was developed during the opening song time.

It is crucial to develop a sense of unity and oneness in camp settings. Group singing fosters community in several ways:

- The group is unified as they direct their collective attention to a designated leader. Because of this, when a speaker is introduced, the focus of attention is already up front.
- As kids come into a meeting—even if they know each other well—they arrive with a wide variety of emotional and social inhibitors that are not easily left behind. As they join in group singing, however, they will have an easier time leaving their problems at the door as they are drawn in to something larger than themselves. Thus, although kids come to a gathering preoccupied with themselves, singing can gradually draw them into a sense of belonging and better enable them to listen and learn.
- Community is built on shared experiences, and singing is one of the easiest to program. Nothing draws a fragmented group together like singing.

It is more difficult than is readily apparent to effectively lead group singing, especially when the group being led is large or diverse. Song leading takes training and practice, but almost anybody with diligence can learn it. A good voice is not a requirement—in fact, some of the best song leaders are also pretty rotten singers! (I have been told that I am a pretty good song leader, and I used to think that I had an almost presentable voice. I did, that is, until my son turned eight and finally leveled with me—"Dad, it's okay if you want to play your guitar and sing to me, but don't quit your day job!")

A good song leader knows these secrets:

- It is unnecessary to lead group singing by singing into a microphone (unless the crowd is over a thousand; then you are *forced* to). Lead with your hands and arms. This will allow the crowd to hear itself singing, instead of feeling as if they are simply "following the leader." It's best to start the song with both your arms and voice, making sure the crowd has the proper key, and then step away from the microphone and keep them together using arm motions.
- As much as possible, get the crowd to keep their eyes on you and not on lyrics in a book or on an overhead. This will unify the crowd's focus (very important for a speaker), keep the song flowing from the front instead of from within the crowd, and help people experience the music rather than concentrate on reading it.
- If you use overheads, it is important to maintain integrity and obtain copyright permission for all of the songs you use. This is a relatively easy and inexpensive process. You will need to plan in advance and write to the publishers who charge a small fee for granting permission. There are even clearing houses that provide youth groups with the service of gaining permissions. But whether you get it directly or through a service, don't neglect to get permission—songwriters need to eat, too!
- Pick songs that have a purpose. For example, early in a week-long outreach camp, it is best to choose songs that are fun and upbeat (you may even use secular songs if they do not contradict the Gospel), and slowly move toward songs that reflect the content of the messages. It is a good idea to check with a speaker before choosing songs in order to connect the song service with the theme of the message.
- The song order may seem obvious, but I've seen the important principle of placing slow, meaningful songs last violated so frequently that it bears mention.
- Let the speaker speak and the songleader lead songs. An occasional brief introduction may be appropriate, but as a rule, let the songs speak for themselves.
- Have the crowd stand up to stretch just before or during

the last song. "The mind can only endure what the seat can bear!"

For groups that do not have the staff to pull off group singing (it *is* getting harder to find guitar players!), it is now possible to purchase cassette, sing-a-long tracks. Dan Carson, a youth minister in Texarkana, Texas,[1] has developed an entire tape library of fun songs and contemporary hymns for use with youth groups. The Christian rock group Petra has a sing-a-long tape (*The Rock Cries Out*, Word Records, 1989) that comes with a songbook and can aid you in worship. Tools like the ones mentioned are especially effective in camp or retreat settings in that normally the biggest problem with sing-a-long tracks is the students' fear of looking foolish. At a camp these barriers are easily dropped and students are far less self-conscious.

Performance

The imitation "Beach Boy" concert at Mount Hermon in 1971 was one of the most exciting nights of my life. Not only was the program fun and entertaining, the finale to the evening has proved to be one of the most moving events of my life. After the "Beach Boys" finished their second encore, the houselights dimmed and out walked a young woman whom I had seen around camp. Her name was Marj Snyder, and she was an up-and-coming Christian recording artist who happened to live at the conference grounds. Marj had a love for Young Life and its approach to reaching kids, and her contribution to the ministry was her music. She used no instrument, but because of the beauty and simplicity of the song and her voice, she held us spellbound. As Marj sang "Amazing Grace," I felt as though I was listening to an angel singing directly to God and that she was allowing me to listen in.

When you want to touch kids' hearts, musical performance is still an incredibly powerful tool. Ten years ago, it was relatively easy to book a band that most kids would enjoy; rock was the style in vogue. But finding a group today, no matter how well-known or popular, that even fifty percent of your kids will tolerate is a real test. I have noticed that youth workers rarely address this problem when they hire a person

---

1 Dan Carson, Carport Sound, 3015 Moores Ln., Texarkana, TX 75503, 214-831-6000

or band to perform. I make it a habit to sit in the back during camp concerts to get a feel for the entire crowd and not just the first few rows. All too often many (and sometimes most!) of the crowd is bored and waiting for the next activity. They may still buy shirts, posters, and albums, but the impact on their lives is often minimal.

Another myth about Christian groups who perform at camps is that they are a significant draw to *fringe kids* (those involved in the youth group on the periphery, but who are not active or even interested, for one reason or another). I believe that certain well-known groups or personalities may draw some kids, but more often than not they are kids so tied into the program that they would probably have gone to the camp if there had been no music at all. It is a huge investment, both programmatically and financially, to hire a band or singer (or magician or weight-lifter or . . .) for a camp. I would like to recommend that you think about a few things:

- It is not necessarily true that the more well known performers are, the better they are received. Often you can find new and less-known groups who would love to come and serve your kids with their music and would be willing to do it for substantially less money than the cost of a better known group. In light of a given camp's purposes, this type of group may work just as well and also be economical.

- Today's kids respond much better to people that they know and spend time with than they do to performers who treat camp situations like any other "gig" and refuse to get involved with campers and staff. Singers like Freddie Langston[2] and James Ward[3] are more concerned about loving kids both on and off stage than they are about performing. I have worked with both types of performers and, in the way kids respond, there is no comparison.

- Because musical tastes vary radically, it is sometimes best to invite a person or group whose style is more

---

2 Freddie Langston, Papa's Dream, P.O. Box 11575, St. Petersburg, Florida 33733, 813-321-7873
3 James Ward, MTD Talent Agency, P.O. Box 7465, Grand Rapids, MI 49510, 616-241-3787

simple and generic (without being too corny or "sixty-ish"!) rather than dealing with everyone's preferences. Marj, for example, had a style just a few years removed from the folk styles of the sixties and would not normally have caught my attention as a high schooler. But because she spent time with us, because we knew her as a person, and because she sang without accompaniment, her music flowed from her heart into ours, without giving any attention to particular tastes—everybody loved her!

- Sometimes your students have the ability to provide quality performances for their peers. But for the students' sakes as well as the camp's, *always screen campers to make sure they are capable.* It can be devastating to have friends and peers snicker and sometimes even laugh at your sour notes or missed beats.

- If at all possible, communicate directly with your performers. Interview them and make sure they know the purpose of the camp or retreat so you can feel confident that their involvement will help fulfill that purpose.

- Try to get as much use out of your performers as possible. Let them perform a song or two at various sessions or even lead the singing a couple of times before they give their concert. If they cannot be at camp for the whole session or for a few days before their concert, arrange for them to arrive at least several hours before their scheduled performance time. And don't let them hide out in their rooms before and after their concert. You are paying them to *minister* to your kids, so make sure in the negotiation stage that they are willing to serve in a way that best suits your kids' needs.

Dances

The stigma surrounding dancing for Christians has, in most cases, begun to erode. There are still several facilities that forbid dancing on their property. (Most of these do allow you to play music for kids to listen and "respond" to; they just don't want it called *dancing*.)

If you choose to use this type of "musical response," here are a few things to consider. To a great many kids (most of whom remain strangely silent as others cry out for a dance), going to a dance is one of the five most frightening events of their young lives, just below lion taming. One of the biggest reasons for avoiding traditional dances is compassion for those students. Our camps (indeed, all of our programs and events) should make students feel safe, warm, and accepted. Kids should be able to come to our program and know that the painful social realities faced elsewhere will not touch them.

A possible solution is to have a *period* dance (i.e., square dance, a "dance through the ages," or a "fifties" or "sixties" dance), utilizing a prepared tape. In this type of dance, everyone dances together, and the issues of partners and ability become less important as kids just have a great time together. This kind of dance, in fact, can be a great gift to those students who fear dances for social reasons—most of them would *love* to go to a dance and have fun like other kids, but they don't for fear of ridicule and rejection. How wonderful to experience the fun of a dance in a safe and controlled environment filled with accepting friends!

One other thought: Unless you have some incredible kids that you trust absolutely, never let students pick the songs—always have an adult who is familiar with kid's music and also has "good old-fashioned horse sense" be in charge of that. Songs like "Good Golly Miss Molly" by Chuck Berry may seem fine until you listen to the lyrics carefully; then you will find that it contains blatantly obscene language. And because many of today's songs contain even more glaringly offensive themes and lyrics, any music played at a camp should be carefully screened.

Background Music

Most camping programs do not allow background music to be played during meals. This policy is important because meals at camp should be used to build and deepen relationships. Music playing in the background, however subdued, can hinder conversation. But there are rare times and carefully designed instances when background music can enhance the purpose of a given meal. For example, some camps may have a theme meal—a "western" night, for example, that is intended to help break down relational barriers and encourage kids to "loosen up." In such a case, lively banjo music or late 1800's music can add significantly to the evening's ambiance. You also might want to use soft, mood music to set the tone for a dress-up dinner held at the end of the week. But again, these times should be rare, and the music should always be used with a specific purpose in mind.

It is important to use background music whenever there is a lull in a program event. Between entertainment skits, for example, is a great time to keep the crowd involved by providing snatches of fun and universal music—famous country tunes, old motown music, songs by Alvin and the Chipmunks, the Beatles, the Beach Boys, etc. Also use this type of background music *during* your games, mixers, and activities to keep energy and excitement high. A very mediocre relay race can become an unbelievably exciting event when the correct song is used as background. Anyone responsible for a camp or retreat program should come prepared with a vast array of cassette tapes to use in these types of settings.

Another time when background music is effective is before and after general-session meetings. Like every other choice we make in camping, tapes should not be chosen indiscriminately and thrown into the cassette player. If a meeting is planned to be lively and upbeat, the music to which kids enter should reflect that feeling. As they leave, music could either be omitted to maintain a reflective mood, or a soft worship song dealing directly with the content of the speaker's message could be played.

Illustrations

Because music is such a dynamic force in the lives of adolescents, we can use it to communicate truth in a deeply touching way. There are two proven ways to do this:

First, during the course of a message, play a popular song while displaying the lyrics on an overhead projector. There are many popular songs that provide tremendous illustrations of what we in the church need to communicate to kids about their relationships with Christ.

Last summer I was scheduled to be the speaker for a month of Young Life outreach camping. I wanted to use current music, but because James Taylor hadn't had a popular album in a few years, I wasn't sure what to pick. When I asked some of the students I work with to give me some suggestions, they weren't much help—none of them agreed! Finally I decided to go to a local music store and buy the three (clean!) top-selling rock albums in Denver. I then listened to each one and chose a song from each, which I made into an overhead. All three songs worked great, and I could tell that the campers appreciated having the Gospel brought home to them in an understandable way, using as illustrations the music *they* listened to every day.

Another way to use popular songs as illustrations is by altering the lyrics. Occasionally you'll come across songs so popular that your kids know every word. When it is a love song with universal appeal, we can redefine the lyrics to communicate the beauty of the relationship God desires to have with us. For example, "Bridge Over Troubled Water" (performed by Simon and Garfunkle) and "Wind Beneath My Wings" (performed by Bette Midler) both contain lyrics that can be directly related to the Gospel.

When you use redefined lyrics, play the song, and instead of putting the lyrics on the overhead, display Scriptures underscoring the biblical principles you are trying to communicate—the kids already know the lyrics by heart; you are simply changing how they interpret those lyrics. This method has two advantages. First, the next time they hear the song, instead of mindlessly singing along with a secular love song, they will remember the Scripture that redefined the song, and they will be consciously drawn to consider the Lord's love for them. And second, they will be sensitized to the fact that if we are open, there are many reminders in everyday things that can draw us to the Lord. In this way we can help students bring together their faith and lifestyle.

The medium of music is a driving force in the lives of kids, and so we must be purposeful as we plan and program the music for our camps and retreats. Music, in any form—group singing, performance, dancing, as background music, and as illustrations—can either draw young people closer to Christ or drive them away. Because this is true, it is vital that we consider every aspect of music and always ask this question: Will using this musical activity or program move my kids closer to the purpose of the camp or further from it? And the same question should be asked as we consider each individual song to be used.

As you seek answers to these questions, the specific philosophies you must hold and the decisions you must make will become more and more clear. ◆

7

◆ ◆ ◆

But Seriously, Folks: How to Use Humor

Every youth worker tells horror stories about times when camp humor got out of control. I have seen hundreds of bad skits, but the memory of one in particular I can't seem to shake.

Dee and I were in Europe speaking at a ski camp for American military dependents. They had the typical campers' "talent show"; some acts were serious, but several cabins decided to do humorous skits.

One guys' cabin chose an old gag that I had seen many times: they modeled their girlfriends' pajamas. I almost left. "I've seen that before," I thought, "I'm going to bed." *I wish I had.*

As the guys came strolling into a room of four hundred high-school peers, they were indeed clad in girls' sleepwear . . . BUT NOTHING ELSE!

I didn't know whether to hide, scream, or get sick. (I won't go into detail, but just think about a group of sixteen- and seventeen-year-old guys wearing tiny panties and *nothing else* . . . .)

Humor is a powerful tool. It can loosen kids up so they have a good time or it can totally undermine what we are trying to accomplish.

If we care for kids, we must never take a casual attitude toward humor.

Philosophy of Christian Humor

When God created humor (or is it simply a facet of his character?) he gave us a great gift.

And, like any gift of value, it can be misused. Any naturally funny person knows the difference between good, solid humor and a cheap laugh. It is easier to get people to laugh at taboo, outrageous, and put-down humor, because people are either so taken aback or so enjoy seeing others ridiculed that they laugh.

But we are in the business of reconciliation, healing, and love. At all costs we have got to steer well clear of things that may offend, hurt, or abuse anyone.

Here are some examples of humor that help kids enjoy life:

- Situational humor that is potentially common to all (e.g., a couple trying to learn to dance to a record).
- A wild characterization of a cartoonish individual (e.g., Steve Martin's "Absent Minded Waiter" skit, in which he is lovable but clutzy).
- Sight gags and magic, as long as they are not abusive, racist, or sexist (e.g., the old "Sumo Wrestlers" skit, in which the contenders never touch but throw themselves and their opponent falls, could be called, "No Touchy Wrestling").
- Lip syncs of bizarre or wild recordings.

And here are some examples of the type of humor to avoid:

- Any ethnic humor where even the slightest degree of offense may be taken.
- Any reference to abuse, whether physical, sexual, or verbal (like the "Saturday Night Live" skit featuring the "Yelling Sergeant").
- Guys dressing up as women (statistics tell us we have a number of young men who secretly struggle with their sexual identity, and this type of humor not only hurts them but pushes them further away from our ministry).
- Sexually suggestive humor, whether explicit or implicit.
- Cheap "bathroom" humor.
- Any put-down references to weight, size, or any other physical characteristic that could damage an already hurting kid.

In Messages

The gift of humor is a much acclaimed and sought after gift. People tend to look up to those who are funny and often want to be like them (I *know* I wasn't the only kid who knew every line of every Bill Cosby routine!). In youth work, we see the attention that funny speakers receive, how confident and clever they appear, and how kids seem to really like them; so, when it is *our* turn to speak, we try to copy that "superstar" who spoke at camp. Sometimes we are able to pull it off, sometimes the crowd is being polite, and sometimes they are downright rude and obnoxious! Many youth workers have been hurt and embarrassed trying to be something or someone they were not.

The key to any effective presentation that has an element of humor is being yourself. Everyone is a *little* funny, but rarely when they are trying to be. Life is filled with humor, and some of the greatest speakers I know have a winsome freshness because they are who they are and don't take themselves too seriously. As they tell stories and anecdotes, the humor flows naturally from the content and is never forced. So, if you want to be light and fun, talk about your own encounters with life, don't take yourself too seriously, and allow the joy of living to come from within as you speak. Kids will be blessed and touched and have a good time.

Some Nuts and Bolts

There are three schools of thought about who should take part in entertainment (skits at camp):
- Kids need a chance to perform in front of their peers.
- As counselors take opportunities to be silly, their students will see them in a different light and thus feel more comfortable with them.
- Only the best performers should be used so that students can have a great time, drop their barriers, and feel special because they were given a dynamic presentation.

Each of these schools of thought has merit, but the best solution is to create an entertainment night combining the best elements of all three. Here are some thoughts on pulling off an unbelievable evening of fun!

Student performances. Watch out! As I watched that awful skit in Europe, I couldn't help thinking that this episode could have been avoided. Any time we give students (or young leaders, for that matter) the freedom to perform, *anything* can happen. We are ultimately responsible for making sure that everything happening at a camp or retreat is well done and congruent with the Gospel. We must never assume that "they'll be fine"; we need to *insist* on auditions and be available just before they go on to make sure they are going to do what we expect them to do (and make sure they'll be wearing what we expect them to wear!). It takes a great deal of planning and work to follow through on these rules, but the results will be well worth the effort.

The best way to monitor camper skits is to require a leader to be directly involved in its performance. Every leader should then be clearly instructed as to what is appropriate and be reminded that they represent Christ and the camp staff as they hold their kids accountable. A great benefit of this approach is that it provides another opportunity for leaders to spend time with their campers.

Counselor performances. Sometimes this is the best overall way to ensure quality and at the same time allow campers to feel included because they know the players. The danger lies in trying to cut corners and not adequately prepare leaders for their roles. The person who can "wing it" and still ensure quality and timing is rare. Almost everyone has to practice a skit to be good, and adequate practice is even more essential as the number of people involved increases. Take time to teach people skits, and then give them time to practice. To make things easier on your volunteers, the camp staff should get the costumes for the counselors and let them spend their time either learning their roles or relating to their kids.

Staff performances. Intricate skits and those requiring careful timing can often take hours of practice. It is unfair (and unwise) to expect counselors to spend a great deal of time preparing to entertain—that is not their primary function. That is why it is a good practice for the staff to have a few solid skits "in the bag" when camp time arrives. Even if the other acts fail miserably, these will be bits you know can make the evening a winner.

Another advantage to staff-performance skits is that they give campers a chance to see the speaker and other camp staffers in a different role. I love to make kids laugh in an entertainment situation, but as a speaker I rarely get the opportunity. Kids seem to feel far more comfortable with me as a person when they have seen me make silly faces in a skit. This pays tremendous dividends when it comes time to challenge kids to make a decision.

One Last Word . . .

I love humor. And humor can aid the communication of the Gospel to young people. But I have also been known to go overboard when I perform or even speak and draw more attention to myself than to Christ. As I've grown older I have discovered that, like most people with the gift of humor, much of what I do comes out of insecurity. It is my lifelong ambition to seek health and security in Jesus Christ, and I seek to use my gift of humor for his sake. As we plan and operate our camps, retreats, and conventions, I pray that we will be able to recognize humor for the "two-sided" gift that it is. We must never let it get in the way of our love for kids. It is too valuable and far too powerful a resource to be taken lightly. ◆

SECTION TWO

HITTING YOUR TARGET

Specialized Camps and Retreats

Now that we've looked at the elements that make a retreat or camp successful, let's focus on specific camp and retreat options. By identifying a specific constituency and a purpose, and by committing an entire retreat to the needs of that group and to that purpose, our youth camping programs can be life changing, regardless of the tools we use.

This section is divided by types of purposes and needs. The chapters have no intended sequence, but nearly all of the chapters follow a set format. If you know what type of camping style will best fit your group's needs, simply turn right to the chapter dealing with it. If you don't know which camping method would be best, first develop a Mission Statement of Vision (see chapter 2, "Developing a Camping Strategy"). When you have your purposes (vision) clearly in mind, use the chart at the end of this chapter to direct you to several camping methods that will fulfill those purposes. Because several camp types may meet the same purposes, they also may suggest the use of some of the same options (e.g., stress and recreational camping have some similar purposes), but when these parallels occur, the elements are listed in both chapters so that each chapter can act as a self-contained unit and be read independently of the other.

You can also use this section to familiarize your volunteers or co-youth workers with the purposes and philosophies of an upcoming event. Have everyone involved in the camp or retreat read the chapter that focuses on your event. Not only will this unite your staff, it will also provide ongoing training for your team.

Each chapter is divided into the following sections:

- *Introduction.* To illustrate a specific camp's value, each chapter begins with a story or illustration based on a camp that has had an impact on my life. Even veterans who are skeptical about the need to plan camps from the bottom up will be able to identify with the anecdotes presented in each chapter.
- *Description.* Each chapter provides a one-paragraph description of a camp type, depicting its unique features and philosophical premises. This description is the foundation on which its purpose will stand.
- *Purpose.* For each chapter more than one purpose is provided because any out-of-the-ordinary experience will have several levels of purpose. In chapter 11 ("Stress

Camping"), for example, three purposes are mentioned: to build community, to build trust relationships with others, and to help kids see and experience Jesus Christ's trustworthiness in every circumstance. These purpose statements make up the philosophical focal points for the camp's goals.

Each purpose statement explains in detail how a specific purpose fits in with the description of the camp. And in this explanation the elements of Section One of this book begin to surface as they are actualized in camping situations. These statements can be valuable as you train camp counselors and other personnel.

- *Goals.* The goals give specific instructions for pulling off each given purpose. This is where each chapter gets really practical—now that a purpose has been fully explained in theory, this goal section takes the purpose statement and translates it into relatively specific action steps.

   Because each camp is different, it would be futile to attempt a detailed list of things to be done to keep the retreat focused. Each goal or action step gives us some idea of what needs to take place to achieve our intended purposes. This section is meant to stimulate creative yet specific thinking, not to tell you precisely how your retreat should look (there are other books and resources available that can tell you exactly what to do, but to make that an emphasis would violate the premise of this book—that you must design every retreat to meet the needs of your group specifically and not rely on canned or cookie-cutter formulas).

- *Options.* This section of each chapter provides possible alternatives to traditional camping formulae. Again, the listing is not intended to be exhaustive—the alternatives are included to stimulate your creative thought processes to meet your group's needs. Only a few of these options are new, or even very creative, but they will help get your creative juices flowing.

- *Possible Schedules.* We must exhibit tremendous flexibility if we want to create a camp that will meet the needs of kids. We can often feel that we are spinning our wheels every time we go to the drawing board. Certain givens need to be addressed—obvious things like eating and sleeping. To help camp planners who are spending a minimum of time and energy creating schedules, each chapter provides a schedule that can serve as a starting point from which any camp or retreat schedule can be planned.

Finally, as you use Section Two to come up with the very best camping programs for your group, please remember that programs should be viewed merely as tools with which to help young people build relationships with Christ and with others. Even the best schedules, programs, and structures must be viewed in this light or they will overshadow kids' needs. Students must be our focus, mission field, and therefore the reason for our ministry program. We have a tremendously high calling—to bring kids face to face with the Lord—and we must fight the urge to rely on programs, creativity, or special abilities as we design our camps, retreats, and conferences.

Listed below are the purpose statements for every option in Section Two:

PURPOSE STATEMENT	TYPE OF CAMP	CHAPTER
To build community through shared experiences	Recreational	10
To build trust and deepen friendships between the staff and the students	Recreational Stress	10 11
To show kids that Jesus Christ can be an integral part of group fun	Recreational	10
To provide students with opportunities for personal spiritual growth	Discipleship	8
To help students see that Christian growth is marked more by footprints than by monuments	Discipleship Service	8 12

PURPOSE STATEMENT	TYPE OF CAMP	CHAPTER
To help students realize that the responsibility for Christian growth is primarily personal	Discipleship Stress Service	8 11 12
To build authentic trust relationships with disinterested kids	Outreach	9
To be like Paul and "preach Christ crucified" (1 Corinthians 1:23)	Outreach	9
To give a nonverbal as well as verbal presentation of the Gospel	Outreach	9
To help kids see that Jesus Christ can be trusted whether life is easy or hard	Stress Service	11 12
To follow the Lord's mandate to serve the needy (Matthew 25:31–46)	Service	12
To instill in student leaders a sense of ownership	Planning	13
To plan group programs in a non-structured environment	Planning	13
To build a deeper commitment to Christ	Discipleship Service Planning	8 12 13

8

Discipleship

A nyone who has worked with adolescents for any length of time has struggled to find the balance between pulling in fringe kids and encouraging the growth of already interested students. As youth workers, we want to continually challenge our core groups, but the idea of devoting an entire retreat to them may seem risky or even absurd. There is an old adage, however, that claims, "Health breeds health." Because this is so, it may sometimes be smarter to focus on our core kids with the hope that it will encourage the others to catch up.

A small group of youth pastors in Colorado gathers to give their leadership (or discipleship) kids a weekend of input and fellowship. Their retreat focuses on growth and service and is not for everybody. It's true that the elements of fun and adventure are involved and that the time is filled with more than Bible studies and discussion groups. But the content, challenge, and expectations go far deeper than at the average youth retreat. The students who have attended this gathering have become the motivational leaders of their youth groups. The weekend has become an annual tradition, and its organizers agree it is the most productive retreat of the year.

A discipleship camp or retreat fits into an overall program of a youth ministry because it takes care of those students who are most in tune with its purposes. As these students are nurtured and developed, they become the leaders in the group—in the program itself and also as peer models living out what is being preached week by week. Groups that do not place a high value on intentional nurture and do not use camps, retreats, and other creative programming means to develop leadership and discipleship students, tend to be stagnant and boring. An essential element of an overall plan is commitment to helping these kids grow and actively pursue their gifts as peer leaders.

Youth programs must be committed to the long-term nurture of these students as well as to reaching fringe kids. As you plan your program, then, whether on an annual or semester basis, allow for meeting the needs of both types of kids. The best way is to plan three or four (at least) yearly retreats, each with a different emphasis.

For example, a fall retreat could be an outreach or fringe-kid event. A winter camp could follow, geared to help students who are ready to learn, be challenged, and grow. Invite the entire youth group, but program for committed students, and expect the others to participate at that level. It might be helpful to let your students know the goals of each retreat, so you are not fighting expectations when you get there.

Description

Discipleship camps and retreats are specifically designed for students who already have some sort of ongoing relationship with Christ. Because of their history either in the youth group or church community, or because of the way in which they are being raised, these students need specific challenges that will facilitate growth in their faith. And because these kids are undemanding and easy to please, we often fail to plan programs that will give them the challenges they need. To fail in this is to miss out on increasing their potential as leaders and to show how narrow our thinking is about the possible uses of camps and retreats. The student that is ready for growth and challenge deserves special attention and directed input.

Purpose

To provide students with opportunities for personal spiritual growth. Every student, regardless of history and commitment, needs to be continually challenged, encouraged, and pushed in his or her walk with Christ. There are many ways to accomplish this; it just takes creative effort, and, for most of us, the willingness to let go of past experiences and expectations. The key is to make sure that the program is directly focused on those students who want to grow. Simply target these students and expect the others to catch up. No matter what tools or specific options are used, the goal must be to let kids face growth head on and meet the challenge. From every angle—the planning, the staff, the kids, the songs, the worship opportunities, the speaker—the goal must be a commitment to stretching students in an effort to stimulate spiritual growth.

Goals

- To choose a topic for the camp geared to helping Christians grow in a specific way. Subjects such as disciplined prayer, meditation, obedience, and financial giving work well.
- To make that topic relevant to the students' daily lives. Apply any input or direction to one of five areas of their lives: family, school, social, interior (their hopes, dreams, fears, etc.), or Kingdom (their relationships with Christ and the church).
- To thoroughly brief the camp speaker on the camp's purpose well in advance and make sure that the purpose is clearly understood. For many speakers this type of emphasis will be a new one.
- To plan seminars that are in tune with the determined purpose. For example, a seminar on sex and dating should be very different at a discipleship camp than at an outreach camp. At a discipleship camp, the seminar should focus on challenging students to "live lives worthy of the Gospel," and should encourage kids to follow Christ in their thought lives as well as in their dating activities. At an outreach camp, the purpose is to help kids see that Jesus Christ loves them as they are; proved it by dying for them; and requires in response a commitment to be repentant in heart, mind, and lifestyle. Discipleship kids need more specific focus and direction in *how* to live out this commitment.
- To develop a schedule that reflects a purposeful commitment to growth and content. It might include seminars, discussions, and spiritual growth videos, for example, where a traditional camp would have more free time. Because students are there to learn more about

their faith and to interact with information that can help them grow, they will be more able to handle a relatively packed schedule than disinterested students would be.

Purpose

To help kids see that Christian growth is marked more by footprints than by monuments. Camps and retreats often give students the impression that the Christian life is the quest to move from one "mountaintop" experience to another. Sometimes we communicate that "true" faith is found only in a special feeling derived from dramatic emotional releases and is usually brought on by intense social times with the community to which they belong.

Young Christians, especially kids going through a discipleship process, need to know that living life as a disciple of Jesus Christ means carrying on an ongoing, everyday relationship, and that retreats are simply times during which we focus on issues that must be concentrated on at home.

For a discipleship retreat to meet this goal, it must be designed around the philosophy that results are not measured by the number of kids making commitments or by the things students say on Sunday morning. The real test of a successful discipleship camp is whether changes are evident in the lives of kids three months after the retreat.

Sharon, Shelley, and Cathy had been involved in our group since they were freshmen, but were still on the fringe. During the discipleship snow camp held in their junior year, they didn't respond overtly. They listened intently to the speaker, but were silent when it came to the all-group sharing on Sunday.

During the weeks following the retreat, though, all three girls began to get more involved. Whenever volunteers were needed, they were the first to raise their hands. During a discussion I held with the group about what we should do on spring break, the girls campaigned hard for a service trip to Mexico (and won!). By the time they were seniors, Sharon, Shelley, and Cathy were the key leaders of the youth group. That discipleship camp had been their turning point; they did not emotionally respond, but because they had been challenged to make thoughtful decisions concerning following Christ in specific areas of their lives, the experience was life changing.

Goals

- To give instruction in bite-sized portions. If kids are to comprehend and apply a necessary facet of dynamic Christian living, we must be careful not to overwhelm them. Many youth workers (myself included), in their desire to see kids learn and grow, sometimes load on expectations that are greater than kids can handle.

  Take the idea of daily quiet times, for example. Many youth workers try to get kids to commit to spending half an hour with Christ every day, when most of us aren't even doing that consistently! We need to avoid producing instant guilt through high expectations and instead provide our kids with realistic goals and growth expectations. Encourage them to spend ten minutes (or five!) with Jesus once a day for a week, and then set up a procedure for accountability. Setting simple, clear goals like this will help kids grow in amazing ways.

- To provide practical suggestions to help kids learn what it means in a practical sense to follow Christ. While it may not touch everyone in the same way, or with the same results, a discipleship retreat or camp should help kids learn what it means to follow Christ where they live. Let's keep in mind the old philosophy of KISS: "Keep It Simple, Stupid!". Too often kids are repeatedly told to be committed but given no idea how to follow that command.

  Mike Yaconelli and his wife, Karla, in their work with a Young Life club in their hometown of Yreka, California, have developed a good tool for helping students incorporate insights gained from a retreat into the fabric of their normal daily schedule once they return home. At the close of a weekend retreat or camp, Mike and Karla distribute to the students a list of possible resolutions they can make to begin to integrate their faith decisions with their daily lifestyle.

  This can be a part of the closing worship service or it can be a part of a quiet time of meditation on the last day of camp.

The list below gives examples of ideas for Post-Retreat Resolutions.[1]

Post-Retreat Resolutions

1. Write your parents a letter of affirmation.
2. Clean up your room for a week without being asked.
3. Give your parents a night off.
4. Clean the entire house while your parents are gone.
5. Clean the garage.
6. Wash your parents' car, inside and out.
7. Mow the lawn.
8. Stack firewood.
9. Take care of your brothers/sisters for a night/weekend and give your parents a vacation.
10. Write your folks a long letter telling them what happened this week/weekend on our retreat.
11. Fix your parents breakfast in bed.
12. Fix dinner for the whole family.
13. Set aside a night when you can visit with your parents uninterrupted.
14. Tell your parents that instead of presents for your birthday, you would like money donated to relief work in a country such as Mexico or Haiti.
15. Stay home for the entire weekend just to be with family (no phone calls, no TV, no radio). Ground yourself.
16. Plan a family picnic.
17. Have a game night with your parents.
18. Clean up the kitchen and do dishes for a week.
19. Do family laundry for a week.
20. Set aside an hour per night for a family activity such as walking, jogging, or tennis.
21. Play no music (walkman, stereo, radio) for one week.
22. Stay off the phone for one week.
23. Plan a romantic night for your parents.
24. Tell your stepparents (in person or in a letter) how neat they are.

---

[1] Taken from Youth Specialties 1989 Resource Seminar.

25. Put signs up welcoming your parents home.
26. Surprise your parents by getting a group of friends together to put on a dinner for parents.
27. Give your parents a coupon book with coupons for many of the things on this list (or think of new ones of your own).
28. Improve your grades one point.
29. The next three times your parents say no to something you want to do, don't argue or pout, just say, "Oh, okay," and nothing else.

The idea is to ask the campers at the end of a discipleship retreat to circle three things they are going to do differently during the next two weeks as a result of the camp. As young people get specific and put their faith into practice in relationships, Jesus will become more real and relevant.

Purpose

To help students realize that the responsibility for Christian growth is primarily personal. I've heard it said that shortly after graduation from church youth-group programs, seventy percent of our students abandon churchgoing. That statistic, if nearly accurate, should awaken all of us in youth ministry to our kids' need to learn how to own their faith. The way that most kids behave during a Sunday morning or evening program is often far from the way they act in other surroundings. Every student who has a desire to know, love, serve, and follow Jesus Christ has to be led to see that, foundationally, they alone are responsible for keeping their faith alive and active.

Too often we spoon feed our kids so they will not struggle too deeply or have to take too much personal responsibility. We spend the majority of our time, money, and efforts on keeping students happy and excited. But where do the Gospels claim that following Jesus is primarily fun and exciting? It is crucial to let adolescents see and experience first-hand the Gospel's teachings on service and suffering; if we expect our instructions to have rich, deep, and life-changing effects, we must give them while our kids are still impressionable. We need to treat our more solid kids as true disciples and not just "kids" waiting to become followers of Christ.

Goals

- To have students actively participate in the retreat programs. If the retreat is on prayer, build into the program several opportunities for students to pray, both publicly and in solitude. If the retreat is on service, don't just teach *about* service, get your kids to actually serve! Program into a chunk of free time an opportunity to serve the property staff (they can always use help): clean cabins or the kitchen, do a building or painting project. Or you might plan your retreat near a state or national park, or an Indian reservation, and take a half day to help out. What you do is not half as important as showing kids you are serious about what you are teaching them.
- To allow the students to own the retreat. Give them opportunities to make decisions about everything, from the schedule to the use of free time to announcement giving. The more you encourage their ownership and participation, the more they will feel as though the experience belongs to them.
- To give students some preparatory "homework" to complete before going to camp and before camp meetings. The more kids do on their own, the more sense of ownership and commitment to their own personal growth they will develop.

Options

One good way to begin building discipleship retreats into a youth group's program on a regular basis is to start off slow and relatively light. Newcomers to intense and long periods of prayer, for example, may find the idea of a prayer retreat imposing (and for some, downright negative). Try beginning with lots of singing, community-building games and exercises, and maybe even a skit or two. Focus the teaching on the topic or tool being used, but expect only a small amount of involvement on the first night and increase your expectations with each session.

Here are some options that have been tried and found effective with students:

Prayer. A prayer retreat is designed to give campers the opportunity to first learn how to pray and then spend significant amounts of time in prayer. The theme of this type of camp should be simple and straightforward—building a desire for prayer, giving a framework and model for prayer, and making a commitment to regular and frequent prayer times.

The goal is for every student to have the chance to practice meditation, worship, intercession, and petition within the environment of the community. This will be a positive beginning for them as they seek to deepen their walk with Christ through prayer.

Silence. The name, "Silent Retreat," can discourage even the most stouthearted youth worker, but it basically refers to a created opportunity to experience the gift of silence. In this busy, fast-paced, noisy world, being programmed to be quiet, even for a short time, is a tremendous gift. Catholics have long known the value of taking time away from the daily grind to be with others in spiritual community and quiet before God, just relaxing and hearing his small, still voice. What better way could there be to help kids who live in an environment of nonstop noise!

As in any discipleship retreat, it is best to start slow and place few expectations on our kids. One way is to begin with short times of meditative silence, then build in small groups to discuss the time. The next step could be taking solitary walks and then enjoying a meal to "let loose" for a while. During the afternoon, there could be some games or events, followed by a short time of community "silence," with occasional readings from the Scriptures interspersed. After the sun goes down, plan for a feast and a celebration of the ways that God has spoken during the day. You might also combine an all-day or half-day fast with an evening celebration and feast.

Topical theme. Usually the issues facing fringe students and our more committed kids are the same. There is a difference, however, in the means we use to encourage them to face an issue. Parental relationships, healthy Christian dating, friendship, drugs and alcohol, R-rated movies, politics, abortion, money, and many other topics can be dealt with in a much more powerful and honest way if students are already commited to Christianity. However these topics are handled—in seminar form or as the focus of an entire retreat—it is important to keep the principles discussed in this chapter foremost in our planning.

Another way to use a topic theme could be to hold a directed and specific "Lifestyle Challenge" retreat. This could even be a title for the yearly discipleship camp, so students would come prepared to be challenged in their Christian lives. You might have your students choose the hot issue to be addressed every year, so they can maintain ownership in the program.

Student-led, student-taught, or a debate. A lot of preparatory work is needed to make this a quality camping option, but the results will be well worth the effort. Many of our leadership students are waiting for a chance to use their gifts. Although they may not have the same skills of a recognized speaker, their message and input will be far more valuable because they are members of the community. Not only will the audience be challenged (if done properly), but the kids presenting the program will have an incredible opportunity to grow as well.

Sample Schedules

WEEKEND DISCIPLESHIP CAMP

Friday

6:00	Leave for retreat.
8:00	Arrive, register, and find rooms.
8:15	Staff and counselors meet to run through schedule.
8:45	Meeting: singing, community-building time (e.g., mixers, games, skits), message.
10:00 (or so)	Free time.
11:00	Lights out (or cabin time).

Saturday

7:30	Staff and counselors meet to pray and plan.
8:30	Breakfast.
10:00	Meeting: singing, community-building time, message.
11:30	Free time (maybe a game or activity).
12:30 (or 1:00)	Lunch.
2:00	Group interaction (e.g., game, activity, discussion, competition).
3:00	Free time.
4:30	Option #1—seminar(s).

Option #2—group meeting.

6:00 (or 6:30) Dinner.

7:30 Meeting: singing, community building, message.

9:30 Free time (or cabin time).

10:30 Group game, discussion, or entertainment (e.g., films, songs).

11:30 Lights out.

Sunday

7:30 Staff and counselors meet to pray and plan.

8:30 Breakfast.

9:30 Clean up and pack.

10:30 Meeting: singing, community-building time, message.
Head leaders check cabins.

12:00 Free time (or cabin time).

12:30 Lunch.

1:15 Leave for home.

WEEK-LONG DISCIPLESHIP CAMP

Day 1

Afternoon Arrive, get settled.

5:00 Staff and counselors meet to run through schedule and pray.

6:00 Dinner.

8:00 Meeting: singing, community-building time, message.

9:30 Free time (maybe a game or activity).

11:00 Cabin time.

12:00 Lights out.

Daily Schedule (with one or two variations)

7:45 A.M. Camp-staff meeting (counselors need not attend); prayer and planning.

8:30 Breakfast.

10:00 Individual or small-group set up.

Discipleship ◆ 97

10:15–11:00   Individual or small-group time.
11:15   Group interaction.
12:30   Lunch.
1:15   Free time (possibly seminars later).
6:00   Dinner.
7:00   Staff and counselors meet to pray and plan.
8:15   Meeting.
9:15   Cabin time (or individual quiet time) followed by group activity (e.g., skits, band).
11:00 (or 12:00)   Lights out.

Alternate Daily Schedule #1—Brunch Day

9:30   Camp Staff meeting: prayer and planning.
10:30   Brunch.
12:00   Seminars (or role play).
1:15   Free time.
4:30   Seminars.
6:00   Dinner.
  Continue with regular daily schedule

Alternate Daily Schedule #2—Wild Evening

  Use regular daily schedule until 5:00 P.M.
5:00   Staff and counselors meet to pray and plan.
6:00   Meeting: singing, message.
7:00   Cabin time.
7:45   Counselors tell kids to dress up.
8:15   Special dinner (fifties, Western, future, etc.): include mood music, singing, costumes, and entertainment.
9:30   Square dance, fifties dance, wild game or activity.
10:30   Late-night swim. ◆

9

♦ ♦ ♦

Outreach

As a sophomore in high school I was invited to my first outreach camp—a Young Life ski camp. No one I knew was going (even the leader who recruited me didn't go!), and I had no idea what I was getting myself into. I had been a nominal churchgoer and was not committed to my youth group or to Christ. I was a perfect candidate for an outreach camp.

But they really blew it; they did everything wrong! There were no counselors assigned to specific kids (at least no one was assigned to *me*), we had no cabin times to discuss the speaker's talks, and there was little or no program. We got up each morning, went an hour away to ski (with whomever we could find, and for me, that was the loneliest part!), came home to a buffet dinner, and finished off the evening with a club meeting and free time. I spent my time in loneliness and boredom and was more than ready to come home.

On the last full day of the trip, when I was ready to call my parents and have them pick me up because I had no one to ski with, the Lord stepped into my life through the person of Dean Borgman, now on the staff of Gordon Conwell Seminary. I had seen him from afar and knew that he was my Young Life leader's brother but had never met him. He saw me standing alone and asked if I would ski with him. Would *I* ski with *him*? Dean spent all day with me (at least that's how I remember it), and introduced me to some other kids who befriended me and made me sit right up in front during the message. When the speaker talked about Jesus calling "Zeke" (Zacchaeus) out of the tree, I knew that Jesus was calling to me, too.

I committed my life to Christ that night, and, while there were many things done wrong at the retreat, two things were done right, and God used them. First, someone came alongside me and loved me just as I was. Within the context of that friendship I was introduced to a new set of friends who loved me like no one else had. Second, the message of Jesus' love was pure and beautiful. Its content was simple and straightforward, yet deeply powerful. These two ingredients blended together in a way that freed me to consider the claims of Christ on my life for the first time. For all they did wrong, I am grateful that God had those camp's leaders focus on relationships and Jesus Christ.

To be true to the description of an outreach event, a significant number of disinterested kids must be attracted. Because evangelism is perhaps one of the most neglected areas of a youth group's ministry, most youth workers lack the ability and know-how needed to execute an effective outreach program.

How does a church program attract fringe kids? There are several ways:

Have a yearly outreach retreat that your own core or active students own and sell to their friends. (Most church students have many friends at school and in their neighborhoods that we never see.) This retreat may need to be the sharpest, most quality experience of the year; if your active students think they might be embarrassed by inviting their friends to a church-sponsored event, they will never again go to bat for the group's programs.

Take your most attractive and popular retreat and turn it into an outreach camp. Take several months to teach your students the value of having an outreach camp, but also let them know the retreat is not for them, but for those they know who are turned off by either the youth group program or church itself. Get your kids to see the value of bringing in new students and teach them that this is the basic reason for the church—to influence the world and care for people who need the touch of a Christian community. If Dean Borgman and the students he introduced me to had not had the vision to lead me to the feet of Christ, I might not have had ears to hear the Gospel that night.

If nothing else works, take your best retreat of the year and only allow those students who bring at least one friend not presently involved in any church to come. This guarantees at least a fifty-fifty split between regular and outreach students.

Join with others who have a proven track record or at least have a desire for outreach camping. Young Life and Youth For Christ groups love to have churches join them in their efforts to reach the disinterested kids in any community. Even other churches who are doing outreach will probably be open to having partners. The task of youth outreach is so overwhelming that many people are finally waking up to the fact that we all need to help each other.

Description

Outreach camps, conferences, and retreats are unique in that the primary purpose of these events is to introduce the participants to the person and work of Jesus Christ. These campers may be fringe students; they often are students who have no real relationship with any church or Christian program at all in which they can feel part of a community in which people truly care for each other.

Some groups, when putting on an outreach event, define outreach as bringing into their own group anyone who is not now associated with *them*. In other words, outreach is defined as reaching into other groups to build their own. But because of the vast numbers of students who are not tied into *any* group, we in youth ministry have a tremendous responsibility to do all we can to pull in kids who have nowhere to go and have never heard, felt, and experienced Christ's love.

An outreach camping event is one of the most powerful and productive tools for reaching disinterested kids. It can provide an atmosphere of fellowship and belonging, a place to consider the content of the Gospel, an opportunity to be loved and respected in a unique way, and a chance to see Christians live out their commitment to Christ in a community environment.

Purpose

To build authentic trust relationships with disinterested kids. One of the rarest commodities in the adolescent world today is trust. A friend who has proved to be worthy of trust is something we all need and constantly seek, but for the adolescent there often is disappointment and disillusionment. It has been said that young people, when checking out an adult who wants to influence them, will ask the question (albeit subconsciously), "Do you like me?"

Many interpret this as an expression of a tough, "cool" kid, but it is more often the response of a kid who has known a lifetime of being burned. Even the most detached kids need friends they can trust, those who love them and accept them for who they are and where they are.

To make an impact on a disinterested, often mistrusting adolescent, it is of primary importance to first establish an honest trust relationship. This takes time and commitment, but, if relationships are not at the foundation of an outreach ministry program, the process of sharing the Gospel and proclaiming the love of Christ will be viewed as manipulation and result in great bitterness. Jim Rayburn, the founder of Young Life, said, "We must win the right to be heard."

Goals

- To be "counselor-centered." Instead of relying on the speaker's ability to communicate (even though that can be very helpful), on the musician's ability to stir kids emotionally, and on the program's ability to draw kids in, place primary emphasis on the counselor's ability and desire to love students as individuals. This means that counselors are the key players in any outreach retreat.

  In a counselor-centered outreach event, the counselors' (or leaders') sole responsibility is to make sure their kids have the greatest weekend of their lives by making them feel respected, loved, empowered to express what *they* think, and encouraged to be themselves. Counselors are not at camp to be in the skits, to be up front, or to participate in the games—though they may do all of these things to build love and trust with their campers—they are there to see that each camper has every opportunity to feel special.

- To design the entire program with the disinterested kid in mind. From the songs (fun, upbeat, and inclusive) to the skits (never embarrassing, degrading, or potentially painful to *any* student) to the treatment they receive in the dining hall and on the playing fields, these young people need to be touched in ways that communicate that they are special, wonderful, and worthy of the highest respect. Competition should be secondary, and those kids most apt to lose or hurt their team should be encouraged to be winners by being made team "kings and queens." During the nightly cabin times, everyone should be asked what he or she thinks, and everything said should be treated with the highest respect.

- To start the camp off with light and nonthreatening messages and become more direct with the Gospel as solid relational foundations of love and trust are developed. The following graph[1] shows how the message, content, and the program interact over the course of a six-day camp. On day one the emphasis is on programming and on building relationships. By day six the emphasis is on content.

%	Day 1	2	3	4	5	6	%
0	Emphasis: Programming and building relationships with kids. Winning a right to be heard.						100
25							75
50							50
75							25
100		Emphasis: Content. Dialogue with kids concerning Jesus Christ.					0

To communicate clearly that the kids' response will in no way affect their relationships to others involved in the youth group. As I understand our role in outreach ministry, we are not called by God to be a "Christian-making machine," but rather we are called to love those outside the body of Christ enough to give them a glimpse of the Savior. The rest of the work belongs to the Holy Spirit. Yes, we should rejoice over every heart that responds, but we must keep in mind that coming

---

1 Developed by the Young Life Training Department. Used by permission.

to a decision to follow Christ is for many a difficult and lengthy process. We must hang in there relationally with those who continue to struggle and even with those who flat-out reject Christ.

Purpose

To be like Paul and "preach Christ crucified" (1 Corinthians 1:23). We owe it to today's adolescents, who have seen firsthand the hypocrisy of Christians, to be so simple and straightforward in our communication that the only issue on which we stand is the person and work of Jesus. We must focus on asking students to examine the Jesus of Scripture—his life, his claims, his interactions with people and nature, his deeds—and then allow them to decide for themselves if he is indeed "the King of kings and Lord of lords" and "the Light of the world."

When given the opportunity to communicate with spiritually disinterested people there is a great temptation to condemn their lifestyles, morals, and lack of values. But what kids need today is to know and follow Jesus Christ. He is the source of true life, value, and the source of our message. "But I, when I am lifted up from the earth, will draw all [people] to myself" (John 12:32). Values, morals, and lifestyles can all change when Jesus Christ becomes Lord, and as we focus on him we shall see great fruit.

Goals

- To use an understandable yet accurate Bible translation. We can't learn what we don't understand, and to the majority of disinterested or unchurched kids the Bible is a mysterious relic. Of course it must be true to the intent of the original, but that leaves anyone responsible for content great flexibility. Make sure the passage you are using is clear to the audience—the New International Version is often a great choice, but the Phillips paraphrase of the New Testament is also excellent for an outreach crowd. And don't be afraid to change some words to make the passage come alive (as long as you stay true to the intent of the writer), or to combine the clearest portion of two different versions. We must communicate clearly so that every student can have the best chance to see Jesus Christ .

- To have speakers give messages as a friend shares a story rather than as a preacher expounds a sermon. When we do simple things like including ourselves as the recipients of a message by saying "me" instead of pointing the verbal finger by saying "you," we communicate volumes. Our illustrations should show that we not only understand and identify with our audience, but that we share their struggles and challenges. Without condescending or diluting the power of the Christian message, we must strive to be winsome as we seek to reach kids.

- To share the basic message of the Gospel. This message has been captured best in Campus Crusade's "Four Spiritual Laws": (1) the person of Christ (What's Jesus like? What did He do? What did He say?), (2) our need for a savior because of sin, (3) the love of God for sinners as expressed on the cross of Jesus Christ, and (4) the need for repentance by committing to following Jesus Christ as Lord. Together, they make up our message to disinterested kids.

Purpose

To give a nonverbal as well as verbal presentation of the Gospel. Almost every young person today has heard bits and pieces of the Gospel. The widespread rejection of our Lord is often a rejection of a *caricature* of Christ rather than of his true character. Most people are suspicious of a faith that sounds great but has very little to support it. The fall of the televangelists and the apparent hypocrisy of numerous Christians in the public arena have soured many kids to the point that they give an almost automatic negative response to anything labeled "Christian." We must let these students *see* Christ as we try to explain what it means to follow him.

One of the most delicate factors in any outreach program is the subtle temptation to create an atmosphere that can emotionally sway kids into making a profession of faith. In my view, this is not authentic, biblical evangelism. Because God respects the rights of these young ones enough to allow them the freedom of uncluttered choice, we, too, should provide programs that allow as much freedom as possible to consider the claims of Christ, with as little emotional manipulation as possible. While there must be some emotion involved in an examination of Christ and his mission (there is great emotion and passion throughout the Scriptures), kids must be given the chance to reflect, to discuss, and to challenge the message they hear.

Goals

- To include in the schedule time for students to "blow off steam," even when we are in the middle of dealing with heavy issues. An evening of intense content (e.g., the message of the cross) may be a good night for a dance or some wild game or entertainment.
- To build in blocks of free time throughout the camp or at least during the last few days. It is important to make free time for those who want to think and talk as well as for those who choose not to.
- To use seminars to provide another angle on the message of Christ. Seminars are a great tool for communicating the hope of the Gospel to disinterested kids. The content of seminars at outreach camps should be different from what is covered in other retreats because their purposes are different. A seminar on sex and dating, for example, should be not so much a specific challenge or call to purity (for without Christ there is little power), but a call to give up selfishness and shallow relationships in light of what God has to offer.
- To be committed to developing individual relationships with students. Every counselor should be trained and skilled in one-on-one relationships, for they are the key factor in an outreach camp. Our motivation in developing individual relationships with students should be for them to both *hear* about Christ and *experience* his touch as they are loved by leaders or Christian students.

Options

You can be very flexible as you create your outreach retreat or camp. The main ingredient, as stated earlier, is a significant (at least fifty percent) number of uninvolved or disinterested kids in attendance. The best way to recruit them is via relationships, both student to student and leader to student. Most kids will not ask, "What are we going to do?", but rather, "Who is going to be there?" There are several types of retreats that will attract these kinds of kids. Here are a few options:

Out of town. For many students, the opportunity to leave town is an exciting prospect. Whether it is a trip to the mountains, the forests, or even to a remote rural setting, getting away is an attractive way to spend a weekend or longer. We used to take upper-middle-class kids to a pig farm, and they *loved* it; it was such a novelty for them! A Christian camp in a wooded setting is probably the best out-of-town experience for kids in that such camps are usually well-maintained, comfortable for kids, have decent food (but be sure to check this out!), and have facilities for both meetings and recreation.

In town. It is a rare student who doesn't jump at the chance to stay in a hotel, and many youth groups and organizations capitalize on that. If it is a bad time of year for an out-of-town adventure, or if the kind of kids you are trying to reach are more likely to come to a hotel in a large city than ride a bus for two or more hours, a hotel may be a good alternative.

Some unique challenges develop when you run an outreach camp at a hotel. Most of the kids you are trying to reach are not willing to subscribe to the same moral choices that committed church kids are used to. Drinking, drugs, sexual promiscuity, and disrespectful behavior often accompany an outreach event at a hotel (if, that is, you have the "right" kind of kids there!). For some reason, if they are in a rural, foreign environment like a Christian camp, these kids are more willing to "play by the rules"—most of the time. But sometimes, when they think they are set free to be college kids on spring break, they go wild.

The way to avoid this is to make sure there is a counselor assigned to *every room*. If that is not possible, have one for every two adjoining rooms, and never allow the door between the two rooms to be closed. If the counselors are well trained and have worked hard at winning a trusted friendship with the campers, there is a far better chance of maintaining control—most kids will not want to do anything to harm the relationship.

Student-led. As in discipleship camping, the best way to promote ownership among leadership students is to give them a chance to serve. An outreach retreat that is planned, organized, administered, and led by peers can be both a tremendous drawing card and a powerful witness to the disinterested. This option requires a great deal of lead time for preparation as well as some specific and directed staff leadership, but the results will significantly outweigh the work involved.

Theme- or issue-oriented. A weekend that has a specific theme can be a drawing card to students. A Christian-sponsored-but-open-to-all-student-leadership-event is a great way to get student leaders from an entire community (or even state or province) to come together and learn more about leadership from a Christian perspective. A "Wise Choices," "How To Handle Stress," or "Sex and Dating" retreat can also attract many unchurched kids because it appeals to a universal need. The important thing to remember is that a Christian camp is only truly Christian when Jesus Christ, not some particular issue, is lifted up. Issues may help focus a group's attention, but for Christians, the central issue in every area is loving and following Jesus Christ.

Sample Schedules

WEEKEND OUTREACH CAMP

Friday

5:00	Leave for retreat (eat dinner on the way).
7:30–8:45	Work crew dresses up and welcomes each vehicle enthusiastically; campers arrive, register, get cabin assignments, and find rooms.
8:30	Staff and counselors meet to run through schedule and pray.
9:00	Meeting: fun, loud music as kids enter room, singing ("up," current songs), community-building time (three or four mixers, audience-participation skit), two or three more mellow Christian songs, message ("The Person of Christ").
10:30	Snack: (move to dining hall) rules, introduce program "theme," tell kids to dress "grubby" for breakfast.
11:15	Cabin time.

12:00   Lights out.

Saturday

7:15   Staff and counselors meet to pray and plan.

8:30   Breakfast, program continues, divide into teams.

9:30   Team meetings.

10:15   Competition.

11:15   Meeting: singing, message ("Sin").

12:15   Cabin time (may be held in alternate rooms).

1:00   Lunch, program introduces "The Big Event".

2:00   Team meetings.

2:30   "Big Event."

3:00   Free time (or optional seminars at 4:30).

5:00   Counselor meeting.

6:00   Dinner, program (give out awards).

8:00   Meeting: singing, message ("Cross").

9:00   Quiet time: every person in camp takes fifteen minutes to be alone and quiet (this has proved effective for several groups with outreach students).

9:15   Cabin time.

10:15   Free time.

10:45   Entertainment (possibly followed by brief, inclusive dance).

11:30   Free time (or dance).

12:00   Return to cabins, lights out.

Sunday

7:30   Staff and counselors meet to pray and plan.

8:30   Breakfast, no program, announce that an offering for less fortunate will be taken at the morning meeting.

9:30   Clean up and pack.

10:30   Meeting: singing (more worshipful songs,

less rowdy), message ("Becoming a Follower of Christ").
Staff checks cabins.

11:30 Cabin time (or school or youth groups gather as a family to share what the weekend has meant).

12:30 Lunch.

1:15   Leave for home.

WEEK-LONG OUTREACH CAMP

Day 1

Afternoon Arrive, get settled.

5:00   Staff and counselors meet to run through schedule and pray.

6:00   Dinner.

8:00   Meeting: singing, community-building time (e.g., mixers, games, skits), message.

9:30   Free time (maybe a game or activity).

11:00 Cabin time.

12:00 Lights out.

Daily Schedule (with one or two variations)

7:45   Camp staff meeting (counselors need not attend): prayer and planning.

8:30   Breakfast, conclude with upbeat program that introduces the day's activity.

10:00 Preparation for activity (either low-key competition or other all-camp experience that builds relationships and community).

10:45 Activity (e.g., games, competition).

12:30 Lunch.

1:15   Free time (informal time for counselors to be with their kids doing things together).

6:00   Dinner.

7:00   Staff and counselors meet to pray and plan.

8:15   Meeting.

9:15   Cabin time (or individual quiet time), followed by group activity (e.g., skits, band).

11:00 (or 12:00)   Lights out (if not earlier); Cabin time
before bed.

Alternate Daily Schedule #1—Brunch Day

9:30   Camp staff meeting: prayer and planning.
10:30   Brunch.
12:00   Seminars (or role play, activity, or free
time).
1:15   Free time.
4:30   Seminars (optional).
6:00   Dinner.
Continue with regular daily schedule.

Alternate Daily Schedule #2—Wild Evening

Same as regular daily schedule until 5:00
P.M.
5:00   Staff and counselors meet to pray and
plan.
6:00   Meeting: singing, message.
7:00   Cabin time.
7:45   Counselors tell kids to dress up.
8:15   Special dinner (e.g., fifties, Western, future): include mood music, singing,
costumes, and entertainment.
9:30   Square dance, fifties dance, or wild game
or activity.
10:30   Late-night swim.
11:30   Lights out. ◆

... ◆ 10

Recreation

You're going to Disneyland for spring break? What about our responsibility to the poor, the needy, and the lonely?" I responded when I heard about this church's youth-group plans.

"We are doing three different missions trips this summer," came the reply, "and our group needs to experience community right now. So, yes, we are going to Disneyland."

Because I knew the leaders of this group well, I felt as though I had a stake in their decision. At first I was surprised, then bothered, and finally angry. But as I talked to this friend who was helping plan the retreat, I became less critical and more interested.

I do firmly believe that we have so few opportunities to take kids away that we must use them wisely, and so I had written off a purely recreational or social retreat as shallow and a waste of time without giving it any real thought. These leaders had worked hard to create an experience they believed their group needed. They felt a camp experience that would attract kids, be fun, and build community would provide an essential boost to a disjointed youth program. Once I understood that, I was able to get excited with them.

But even a social or recreational retreat must be thoroughly planned and led to fulfill the purposes of the retreat.

Description

A recreational (or social) retreat is any trip or outing that has as its focus an exciting and adventurous group activity. From trips to Disneyland or the beach to water skiing, rafting, or rock climbing, recreational retreats are usually viewed as social times for kids to get away and have fun together. As with any retreat or camp, however, it is necessary to have a clear and defined purpose and set of goals that dictate the program and experience for the group.

Purpose

To build community through shared experiences. Kids today have few places where they "belong." From the time they hit junior high, young people are taught that the world is an unstable environment in a constant state of change.

Too many teachers, coaches, and friends are a reminder to kids that they are unlovely and unlikable. In many families, no time is invested in the building of a much needed and desired sense of community; everyone is simply too busy. Even in their deepest friendships, adolescents spend very little time talking or sharing common experiences that are fun, exciting, and challenging. On the outside they may seem fine, but most kids today are crying out for love, acceptance, and community.

The greatest need in our kids' lives is for situations and opportunities where they can enjoy plain, old-fashioned fun within the context of a "safe" social group. As leaders in the church, we need to help our kids learn what it means to simply "be" in our relationships with each other. Going to the movies or parties will always finish a bleak second to an adventure with a group of friends who care.

As we build programs, camps, and retreats where kids will do things together, where they will be able take time to just hang with each other and talk about the experience they are sharing, a sense of community and belonging to a group will naturally develop.

Goals

- To prayerfully think through our housing list. If the group is large enough to be housed in cabins or rooms, this is essential. While the majority of students may do fine without being assigned, some students will need extra attention. There are many kids for whom it will be a gift just to know they don't have to find their own roommate. By carefully observing the needs of our kids, we can find many ways to help young people feel more included.

- To have opportunities, at least daily, for the group to

talk together, either formally or informally. As students share what they are getting out of the time, or how they are feeling about the experience, the group is forced to listen to and deal with every person, instead of ignoring those who aren't immediately accepted.

- To build community by intentionally focusing on group mixing, specially designed to draw in kids who don't naturally want to mingle.

A way to accomplish this is to have some sort of team or "buddy" system every day that mingles the students throughout the camp. If this fits the type of retreat you are doing, either have two different cabins or rooms assigned to tasks like washing dishes and collecting money, or split up the students into different teams daily and give them a competitive exercise that must be completed before dinner. At Disneyland, for example, divide the group into teams and carry on a polaroid scavenger hunt throughout the day. Leaders committed to building community will keep their eyes open for chances to get the students together.

Purpose

To build trust and deepen friendships between the staff and the students. In the lives of adolescents, friendships with adults are rare. At almost every turn kids feel pushed, pulled, lied to, yelled at, left out, and put down. This is partially due to growing up in a culture that places greater value on results than processes and to the selfishness that has surrounded them since birth. In any case, most young people are leery of adults who claim to be committed to them and love them unconditionally.

In light of this, a recreational retreat can do wonders to bring together students and adults. As kids spend hours or days with adults who care about them, they see for themselves how committed those adults really are. Sitting on the beach talking, standing quietly by a river at night, laughing together at a skit or joke—these types of experiences build more trust and intimacy than a year's worth of youth group meetings.

Goals

- To assign every leader a group of kids for whom their primary responsibility is to help them experience love and community. Ideally, a leader should have no more than eight kids to work with.
- To have leaders spend at least half an hour each day with every kid in their rooms or assigned groups. We naturally drift toward other leaders, the kids we feel more comfortable with, or campers of the opposite sex. These tendencies can completely defeat the purpose of this type of camp, and leaders (including those in charge) should remind themselves daily that the reason they are there is to spend quality and quantity time with kids.
- To have leaders share up-front responsibilities so the kids get to know every leader. Things like giving announcements, collecting money, leading songs, and leading discussions should all be shared at this type of retreat.

Purpose

To show kids that Jesus Christ can be an integral part of group fun. For many people life has become compartmentalized. Their minds are divided neatly into little "rooms." Work occupies a certain space, home another, leisure another, and so on. This is even more true for adolescents, especially when it comes to their faith. "Religion" is something that a large percentage of kids still buy into, and yet even the most active church attenders rarely have a lifestyle that matches their faith. Kids have a hard time seeing Jesus Christ as relevant in their world. We youth ministers must work overtime to address this misconception. We need to help young people see that it is possible to love Jesus and to have fun doing it.

The biggest mistake we can make running this kind of retreat is to fail to program content on which to focus the time. Without some break to hear about Jesus and a specific challenge to consider and follow him, I believe we have wasted not only our time but an ordained opportunity to reach kids. This emphasis does not need to be lengthy, heavy, or even programmed, but failing to come together as Christians as an ingredient in our program pushes kids to further compartmentalize their faith.

Goals

- To have an organized, daily quiet time. Make sure kids are up early enough to take at least fifteen minutes to privately look at a passage of Scripture, pray, and reflect. The best way to do this is to give each kid a notebook at the beginning of the trip that is theirs for the rest of the time. It can match the theme of the retreat (a study on the Kingdom of God could be titled, "Understanding the *REAL* Magic Kingdom!").
- To pray before every meal, even in small groups. The only possible exception to this might be when a large group of kids is eating in a public restaurant.
- To have, if at all possible, some sort of worship gathering every day. Take time to sing, share, focus on a passage of Scripture, and pray together.
- To express our love for and excitement about Jesus Christ in everyday conversation. We need to make sure that counselors are trained and prepared to allow their love for and excitement about Jesus Christ to flow naturally in informal settings. Around a table, waiting for a ride, sitting by a stream, and listening to music can all spark a discussion about the gift of friendship with God through Christ.

Options

Rather than expound on the obvious, here is a list of possible recreational and social retreat ideas:

RECREATIONAL

- Rafting
- Camping and/or hiking
- Sailing—fresh water or small boat
- Fishing (deep sea or fresh water)
- Biking

- Sports camping (either on your own or at a sports camp)
- Houseboat trip
- Snow or water skiing

SOCIAL

- Major amusement park (e.g., Disneyland, Six Flags, water parks, etc.)
- Trip to the beach
- A professional (or collegiate) athletic event out of town
- College "hunting"
- Visit another city or even another culture (like California, for instance!)
- See a play
- Go to a large zoo

Sample Schedules

Because events so often dictate the schedule, the following schedules are divided into two broad categories: recreational retreat schedules and social retreat schedules.

WEEKEND RETREAT
(Snow skiing)

Friday

5:00 Leave for retreat (eat dinner on the way).
8:00 Arrive and set up housing.
9:30 Meeting: singing, brief message (on the purpose of the time and including Scripture), and announcements.
11:00 Lights out.

Saturday

6:30 Wake up, dress for day.
7:15 Breakfast, announcements.
8:00 Gather for morning quiet time (unless it is an outreach retreat, then skip this) load gear, and send the students off on their own.

8:30	Leave for the slopes.
9:00–4:00	Ski or play at the mountain.
4:00	Pack bus, head back.
6:00	Dinner, announcements.
7:00	Staff and counselors meet to pray and plan.
7:45	Meeting: singing, community-building time (e.g., mixers, skits), message or sharing time.
9:00	Free time.
10:15	Cabin time.
11:00	Lights out.

Sunday

6:30	Wake up, clean rooms, dress for the day.
7:30	Breakfast (staff checks to make sure rooms are clean).
8:15	Gather for morning quiet time.
8:45	Load gear.
9:00	Leave for the slopes.
9:30–3:00	Ski or play at the mountain.
3:00	Pack bus and return home.

FOUR- OR FIVE-DAY RETREAT
(Disneyland, or similar theme park)

Day 1

	Depart in time to arrive by the late afternoon.
5:00 P.M.	Arrive, get settled.
6:00	Dinner.
7:00	Staff and counselors meet to run through schedule and pray.
8:00	Gather for either an "official" meeting or a time to do something that builds community (e.g., game).
9:30	Video (or bed, depending on length of trip).
11:30	Cabin time.

12:00   Lights out.

Days 2, 3, 4*

8:00   Breakfast.
8:45   Quiet time: gather to explain quiet time format and send out individually.
9:30   Leave for park.
5:30   Dinner: Meet together to eat.
9:00   Head back to hotel.
9:45   Meeting: formal or informal; use for sharing time (sing? message?).
11:00   Cabin time.
11:45   Lights out.

* Day 4—Optional Schedule

10:00   Breakfast (brunch?).
10:45   Quiet time.
11:15   Pack rooms to leave.
        Gather for message and/or sharing time.
12:15   Check out and leave for park.
5:00   Dinner: Meet together to eat.
6:00   Stay together at park until closing.
12:00 A.M.   Leave for home.

Day 5

8:30   Breakfast.
9:15   Quiet time.
9:45   Clean rooms.
10:15   Check out and head for park.
4:00   Leave for home. ◆

11

. . . ◆

Stress

O kay, I admit it! In over fifteen years of youth ministry I have never been backpacking with a group of kids—or with *anyone*, for that matter. In fact, my idea of "roughing it" is a room in a Motel 6 from which you can hear the freeway! But I *have* been on a few trips that could be referred to as stress camping.

My wife, Dee, was seven months pregnant with our first child when we decided to take a group of eight kids and some leaders on a two-week motor home and sailing trip into Canada. We left Southern California early one June morning and crossed the Mojave Desert around lunchtime. Just before we reached Baker, California (oh, what an appropriate name!), the air conditioner broke down, making the temperature inside even hotter than the one outside—127 degrees. We broke the door, ran dangerously low on oil several times, got lost, and argued—all before we even reached Canada!

The day we arrived in Vancouver, B.C., to meet our boat was beautiful—seventy-five degrees and sunny. The first two days were fun and exciting. On the third day, however, as we were crossing the Straight of Georgia with one of the more inexperienced sailors in our group at the helm, a huge gust of wind filled the sail of our fifty-two footer, and we nearly capsized! I was by the mast securing some line, and my feet went into the water as I was holding onto the mast for dear life! (I heard later that it was far worse down below—the cook was making oatmeal and . . . you can figure it out.) The next day it rained and the "tireds" began to set in. There were some tense moments—having thirteen people in close quarters started to affect us all. By the end of the trip we were all ready to go home.

I'll never forget that trip. Nine years later Dee and I have some very close friends as a result of those two weeks. We spent a solid block of time together, were hot, cold, wet, tired, and everything in between together. In retrospect, those two weeks were perhaps the greatest of our ministry. It may not sound like a stress camping situation to you, but I believe that trips like that, which have enough struggle and adversity to either draw people together or drive them apart, are exactly what stress camps should be.

Stress camps can be rewarding times with kids, but let me give one word of caution: *Never attempt to run a stress camp without professional assistance!* Even if you have some experience in a certain area, experience alone can not ensure that the trip will be consistently safe. Unless you have experience as a professional guide or are licensed in the chosen activity, hire a professional guide or a company to lead your group. Most are very flexible and will allow you to choose your route, timing, schedule, and task assignments while they make sure the trip goes as smoothly as possible. This is not the type of camp for "winging it."

Description

A Stress Camp is any retreat that forces a group to do something together that is uncomfortable and/or stretching. The activity does not have to be something inherently painful or difficult, but it should have elements of risk, adventure, and struggle.

Purpose

To build community through shared experiences. While many youth programs attempt to attract and capture kids by developing snappy and creative programs, the greatest attraction for most kids is the provision of a relational place of refuge. Every young person wants and needs a community where they feel needed. A vast majority of kids have no place like that—not at school, with friends, or even at home. By offering kids programs that give them the chance to experience genuine Christian community, we accomplish more than we could in a semester's worth of banana nights!

Stress-oriented camps, like recreational retreats, are designed to bond students together. But unlike recreational retreats, stress-oriented camps rarely need programming to make community happen—the strains of being physically challenged are almost always enough to bring kids together. But community doesn't just happen because kids are thrown together in a stressful situation. For a group to learn something from an experience, it will need purposeful direction from its leaders.

Goals

- To have daily devotions that focus on Jesus Christ and on current situations the group is facing. Always use Scripture and encourage the kids to read the passage for themselves beforehand.
- To pray together every day and twice a day if possible. Pray for each other; pray for attitudes; pray for safety; pray for insight and wisdom during the day; and make sure there is a healthy dose of praise for the wonder and gift of creation.
- To have a daily sharing time to debrief the experience while you are still in the middle of it. The best time to do this is at night, and then close with a time of prayer and/or meditation.
- To be on the lookout for kids who are discouraged and for those who feel alienated, frightened, or negative. Deal with these adolescents one on one as soon as possible. Especially in a stress camp environment, these elements can destroy group morale and the experience's impact. But solid, immediate leadership can bring the group even closer together.

Purpose

To build trust and deepen friendships between the staff and the students. As kids spend days with adults who are going through a pressure-loaded ordeal simply because they care about them, they are able to see for themselves how committed those adults are to being their friends. Wildly rapelling down a cliff; screaming as your fifty-foot sloop keels over in thirty-knot winds; laughing together in a tiny tent on the third straight day of driving rains; praying for safety during a blizzard; needing help to get across a river—these kinds of experiences cannot help but build trust.

Another way a stress camp builds trust is that it provides opportunities for leaders to serve kids in tangible ways. By definition this type of camping experience causes students to sometimes feel out of control and uncomfortable, so a strong and encouraging counselor who offers leadership, guidance, and assistance to the team wins instant and significant loyalty. This loyalty is a tremendous asset when that same leader shares Christ with kids, because he or she has won a relational platform from which to love and lead.

The key, then, is for the leaders to be well prepared to have their leadership and modeling observed "under fire." The more our leaders are prepared to go and serve, the better they will be able to care for kids.

Goals

- To respond to circumstances with a positive attitude, modeling for students the right reaction to stressful situations. Be aware of how we as leaders respond to circumstances and people, thus setting the tone for the entire group.
- To get in shape with our kids before heading out on a stress camp. Leaders must develop stamina prior to the camping experience; it is very difficult to push a kid further than we are willing or able to go ourselves.
- To verbally exhibit our faith in Jesus Christ as we face opportunities to trust and praise him. It is important for kids to see how we respond to the wonder of creation and to the stress of unforeseen circumstances.
- To care for our kids openly. The genuineness of our compassion for each member of the party cannot be hidden, no matter how hard we try. Whether or not we truly love our kids will come out.
- To de-emphasize competition and emphasize team work. Stress camps separate the sharp and athletic from the slow and clumsy, and how we treat those who fall behind or fail will not only set the tone for the "stars," it will also communicate how important performance is in our relationships with kids.
- To maintain an attitude of encouragement. There is a

fine line between "Marine-like" motivational techniques and Christian encouragement. If we err, let us err in the direction of compassionate encouragement.

- To model spiritual discipline. If we want kids to be consistent in prayer, meditation, and Scripture reading, we must be disciplined as we model it for them.

Purpose

To help kids see that Jesus Christ can be trusted whether life is easy or hard. Unless you work in an impoverished urban or rural setting, the odds are good that most of your students have had few stretching experiences in their short lives. Kids today seem to be lazier and more selfish, even ones who sincerely desire to follow Christ. A stress camp is one of the best ways to push students to rely on others, to force them to "carry their own loads" (often quite literally!), and to function out of the realm of comfort. This kind of setting forces kids to face their self-centeredness and their need for comfort, and at the same time encourages them in their faith. As we place students in uncomfortable situations, ones in which they must try things they never thought accomplishable and in which they need each other to make progress, we give them opportunities to experience Christ's trustworthiness in difficult conditions.

Goals

- To seize the teachable moment. Leadership becomes extremely necessary in a stress camp when the pressure of being uncomfortable begins to divide the group. When one person is whining or being bossy or demanding, there is often a tendency for the group to gang up on that person and even verbally attack him or her. The leaders must deal with offenders as soon as trouble begins, helping them to personally seek God's help and strength.
- To have nightly sharing times. Leaders should constantly observe the *group process* (nonverbal communication, verbal communication, and anything that affects how the members of the group relate to one another), looking for common threads that can be talked about each night.

Rarely are problems and issues kept secret, for in stress situations the body is forced to function as a unit, because "when one member suffers, all suffer"! As the group members deal with each other and are led to discuss and deal with their feelings, jealousies, and frustrations they are forced to both learn about and experience Christian community. They can't go home when this part of the lesson is over! They still have to work *through* difficult circumstances and *with* difficult people.

- To have *every* student and *every* leader keep a journal focussed on the spiritual lessons they learn on the trip. As kids (and leaders) encounter struggles and spend up to an hour a day in prayer and journal keeping, the Lord will be able to speak to them in ways they will always remember.

Options

Stress camps are similar to recreational camps (chapter 10) in many ways, and therefore many of the options are the same. The distinction, however, is that stress camps should concentrate on elements that cause kids to feel discomfort and the need to rely on others and on Jesus Christ. With that in mind, here are some possible stress-camp ideas:

- White-water rafting
- Mountain climbing
- Rock climbing
- Backpacking
- Sailing
- Long-distance biking
- Horseback riding (e.g., at a ranch in Colorado or Wyoming)
- Cross-country skiing

Sample Schedules

Most stress camps usually last a week or more because it takes more than a weekend to make them worthwhile. But there are mini-trips that are excellent warm-ups for a week-long stress camping adventure. (For example, it is very smart to go on one or two weekend biking trips before attempting a long-distance excursion lasting a week.)

WEEKEND "MINI-STRESS CAMP"
(bike trip)*

Friday

5:00	Leave for retreat.
6:00	Arrive at base camp site, set up camp, make dinner as a team.
7:30	Dinner.
8:15	Clean up (together).
9:00	Gather to sing, express fears and feelings, look at Scripture to focus on the purpose of the trip, and pray together.
10:30	Lights out.

Saturday

6:00	Wake up and make breakfast.
6:30	Clean up and stow camp.
7:00	Check equipment and depart.
11:00	Meet advance truck for an hour-and-one-half break and lunch.
12:30	Head back to base camp.
4:30	Arrive at base camp, rest.
5:30	Cook dinner, check and repair equipment.
6:30	Dinner.
7:15	Clean up.
8:00	Gather to sing, share how the day went, take some time to look at some applicable Scripture, and pray.
10:00	Bed or quiet talking.
11:00	Lights out.

Sunday

6:00	Wake up and make breakfast.
6:30	Clean up and dismantle camp.
7:00	Check equipment and depart.

11:30 Meet advance truck, lunch, pack equipment, and head home.

WEEK-LONG STRESS CAMP
(large-craft sailing)*

Day 1

Early- to mid-
morning Leave for the dock.
10:30 A.M. Load the boat.
11:30 Some crew members stow gear below while others make lunch (all kids and leaders, except for the skipper or whoever is in charge, are considered crew members).
12:00 Lunch.
12:30 Finish morning tasks and lunch clean up.
1:00 Explain essential information.
2:00 Leave the dock, sail for the afternoon, assign crew into three teams that will rotate the following tasks daily: galley (meals), deck, and navigation (including helm).
4:00 Continue with nightly schedule.
(Follow every daily schedule with nightly schedule at 4:30 P.M.)

Nightly Schedule

4:30 Anchor for the night, galley crew begins work, deck crew cleans topside, navigation crew determines destination for the next day and plots course and time for setting sail.
6:00 Dinner (served and cleaned up by galley crew).
7:30 Gather for sharing, singing (if it will not disturb others), message or scriptural focus, and prayer.
9:00 Game below deck or time for quiet talk topside.

11:00   Lights out.

Daily Schedule

7:30   Wake up, galley crew makes breakfast, navigation crew double-checks figures, deck crew prepares topside for day's sail.

8:15   Breakfast.

9:00   Quiet time (if desired or not in a hurry, time to gather and discuss the quiet time).

10:00   Galley crew cleans up from breakfast, deck crew lifts anchor and prepares sails, navigation crew heads to a new anchorage.

10:30   Rotate crews, galley crew begins meal preparation, navigation crew rechecks heading, deck crew cleans boat.

12:30   Lunch.

2:00   Option #1: Give everyone free time to read, sing, or take the helm, with the navigation crew keeping an eye on the heading.
Option #2: Head into a cove to swim or "halyard fly" (rig a rope swing) to play as a group.
Option #3: Move into an unplanned but more difficult (or less difficult) sailing situation, depending on the needs of the crew.
Option #4: Anchor early and explore an inland lake or take an impromptu shower in a natural waterfall.

4:30   Continue with nightly schedule.

Final Morning Schedule

7:00   Wake up and start breakfast.

7:45   Breakfast.

8:15   Quiet time.

9:00   Lift anchor and head home, cleaning the boat inside and out.

12:00   Arrive in port.

* REMEMBER: Always have either a professional guide or company handle the safety and liability features of the trip, OR make sure that whoever is in charge meets *all* of the following criteria: has documented and professional experience in the type of adventure you are doing, has experience in that particular route and area, and has the written authorization and verbal confidence of the parents. Don't even attempt to do a stress camp without taking these precautions! ◆

◆ ◆ ◆ 12

Service

Ridge Burns, director of the Center for Student Missions in San Juan Capistrano, California, tells an amazing story he heard from a homeless man in downtown Los Angeles:

Two years ago a youth group came into Los Angeles to work with the homeless. Members of the youth group, in their own timid way, ministered to the men, women, and children of skid row. One night as the youth group was passing out sandwiches to the people around a fire barrel on Wall Street, one of the high school girls in the group gave a sandwich to a man. When he asked her why she was giving him food, the girl became embarrassed at being expected to carry on a conversation with a man of the streets. She had expected to give the man a sandwich and quietly leave. She said that she wanted to help and that this was the only way she knew to be of service. The man continued to prod her, trying to discover her motivation, and soon the Lord was brought into the conversation. As the girl gained confidence, she asked the man about his life and why he lived on the street.

It turned out that the man was a Vietnam veteran and, in fact, a doctor and graduate of the University of Southern California. While in Vietnam he had saved the lives of many American servicemen. Upon his return to the States he felt unwelcome and discriminated against because he had been part of an unpopular war. The pain of what he had seen in the war linked with the stigma he felt upon his return drove him to the streets. He intentionally dropped out of society and began living on the streets of Los Angeles, surviving on his VA pension.

After telling the high school girl his story, this man asked her to explain how he could get to know her God. She went through "The Four Spiritual Laws" with him, and he prayed that night, surrendering his life to Jesus Christ.

The man's life was changed. He decided to continue living on the streets and to begin helping the homeless with his medical skills. Today he lives in a box and carries a medical bag as he helps his fellow street people. His bitterness about the war is gone; now he wants to help make society a better place because "That's what Jesus would do." This man's life was changed by one high-school girl doing the work of the Lord. Kids can make a difference![1]

Our love for Christ is only as big as our love for our neighbors. A service or missions retreat is perhaps the best way to help kids realize that God calls us to a life of service. As they go on a short-term mission or service trip, we should encourage them to view the experience *not* as a one-time event, but as a learning experience that can open their eyes to the needs right before them—in their homes, schools, neighborhoods, and communities.

Leading experts in missions and service agree that helping young people develop a commitment to a lifestyle of service is a three-step process: cultivating an awareness that there is a need, giving short-term exposure to missions and service, and promoting a lifestyle of serving others.

The first step is to make kids aware that there are people with needs outside of themselves. Teaching the importance of reaching out to those in need in Sunday school or Bible-study situations is a beginning, but only a beginning. To encourage kids to open their eyes, we should program activities and events that will force them to deal with the situations of others. For example, during any type of retreat, you could have the students sleep out of doors in boxes for at least an hour, and maybe all night. Or stop off on the way to a camp or retreat and tour a homeless center or visit an impoverished church or poor area.

---

1 Adapted from *The Complete Student Missions Handbook*. Copyright © 1990 by Youth Specialties. Used by permission.

There are many ways to increase our students' awareness, but that awareness must be created before we take our students on a service retreat or camp.

Description

A service retreat (or missions trip) is a retreat primarily devoted to aiding people in need. It can include building houses, cleaning churches, working with the homeless, helping in a feeding program, and assisting an inner-city school or Bible camp (although it is debatable whether simply singing songs and sharing testimonies actually qualifies as a service retreat). There should be some elements of struggle and sacrifice and a willingness to go as learners as well as helpers.

Purpose

To follow the Lord's mandate to serve the needy (Matthew 25:31–46). There has been great theological debate over the exact meaning of Jesus' words, but the Lord's basic point is that anyone who claims to love him has no choice but to actualize that love by caring for others, especially the needy among us. Too often the message we give to adolescents is that they should accept Jesus because *they* will be the beneficiaries of a tremendous life. Although this is technically an accurate description of a element of biblical faith, it is easy for hearers of this type of message to miss the cost of those benefits—the Lord's call to sacrifice, commitment, and suffering. Our students need programs and retreats for which they are not the focus—where they can get dirty and tired and sore, and even to know that their only reward may be in heaven. It is imperative for youth leaders to bring students face to face with their desires for selfish comfort, and a service retreat is one of the best methods for teaching that.

Goals

- To keep service as the primary purpose of the event because Jesus was willing to serve us. Christ must be the focus, not how wonderful our kids are for helping others. This will keep the group properly focused.
- To teach students to be sensitive to the culture in which they are working and then supervise them carefully. Help

them to work diligently to keep from being culturally offensive to the people they have come to serve.

A friend of mine took her youth group to Mexico to work with families who were building the houses in which they were going to live. During the week, temperatures reached into the 100s, and several girls wore halter tops and short shorts. This was more than offensive to the people of the community—to them it was *decadent!* Once confronted, the girls were indignant and it took the entire week for the group to get over that one incident. It was, however, the greatest point of growth for the youth group—they had to learn what it meant to serve Christ cross-culturally!

- To make sure that leisure activities do not conflict with the intent of the trip. Last year a group took kids to Mexico just below the New Mexican border, and on a break a young leader took a bunch of guys to a bar to drink beer. Not only were the parents upset (and rightly so!), the impact that the trip made on the students was also greatly limited.

Purpose

To build community through shared experiences. Community is one of the most vital needs that young people have. To have a place to go where they feel welcome, encouraged, esteemed, and loved for who they *are* and not what they *do* or how they *look* is perhaps the most driving need inside kids today. When a youth group starts focusing outside themselves and their struggles and problems (which are often relatively petty) and begins to serve others as a unit, an amazing transformation occurs—those students who once felt insignificant or on the fringe will develop an identity with the group that could occur in no other setting.

Goals

- To place together kids who would not normally interrelate by assigning prayer partners or triads.
- To look at Scripture together every morning and every

night as a reminder to the group of the reason they are serving.

- To have daily sharing times during which kids can express both the things they enjoy and learn about their frustrations. Help kids to encourage one another in their growth.
- To force students to become acquainted while traveling. Playing mixers is a fun way to accomplish this goal. Think of questions the kids can answer only by conversing with several different people. Make a game out of the trip by getting kids to fill out "Bingo" cards that describe attributes of different people in the group.
- To sing and praise the Lord together. You can hold a worship service as a group or even put one on for the people you are serving.

The above activities will not only aid in building community in the group, they will also help students develop a sense of trust and friendship with their leaders. There are, however, some things to be aware of to ensure growing relationships between students and leaders:

- Assign every leader to a group of kids for whom they will be responsible (see appendix A for instructions on training leaders). Have them make sure that every student feels valued and is growing. They should act as the liaison between the leadership of the event and the campers.
- Have the leaders sleep, eat, and play with the students to build relationships.
- Make sure the leaders work at least as hard as the students. The harder a leader works, the more the kids will respect him or her.

Purpose

To help kids see that Jesus Christ can be trusted whether life is easy or hard. As difficult as a service or mission trip can be, the harder the work, the greater the chance that the experience will be influential and life-changing. Many Christians today have a hard time trusting Christ when life gets difficult. Somehow our warped theology has convinced us that God owes us comfort and ease, when the New Testament in fact assures us that as believers we can expect the opposite. But as we position students to serve sacrificially, to try things they never thought accomplishable, and to rely on each other to make progress, we are giving them the opportunity to trust Christ under difficult conditions and to live by faith in community.

During a missions or service retreat, the work may not be the only thing that makes the trip so difficult. Sometimes there is adversity or a perceived lack of gratefulness on the part of those being served. So we must help kids see that even when we are not appreciated, we are called to serve a hurting world in the name of Christ. Countless kids have come face to face with unrewarded sacrifice in missions settings, and God has deeply touched them by granting a deeper understanding of grace.

Goals

- To work hard at not short-circuiting our students' struggle processes. Sometimes a student will legitimately need a break, but often they are just not used to difficult labor. If we are too easy on our students we may be keeping them from breaking through that "wall of selfishness" that keeps them from having a serving ministry at home.
- To prepare kids in advance for the struggles they will face. We need to spend a great deal of time prior to a missions trip exposing kids to the hardships that can be expected to arise. Schedule short "mini-trips," teach suffering in meetings, and show slides and videos of the type of trip they will be going on. The better prepared our students are, the more able they will be to handle the rigors they will face.
- To give opportunites during every evening of the trip for kids to share the struggles they are going through and to have others pray for them.

Options

The options for getting kids in a position to serve others are countless. But remember one important thing: Do your best to team up with a well-respected local church or organization. This will tend to make those being served feel less like charity cases.

Inner-city service

- Working in an inner-city church, providing materials for renovation, cleaning, painting, etc. (A good option is to work in partnership with that church's youth group.)
- Spending the night or weekend assisting in a soup kitchen or homeless shelter.
- Assisting in an inner-city construction project by rebuilding and/or renovating homes, churches, businesses, etc.
- Holding a camp for underprivileged kids, either locally or out of town.
- Offering to do work projects for an inner-city school district.
- Organizing and running a weekend sports tournament (i.e., softball, basketball, etc.) for inner-city youth, and include free T-shirts, lunches, and prizes for everyone. Supply the funds needed to run a free tournament, including money needed for referees, court or field fees, and refreshments. Conclude with a short evangelistic meeting put on by inner-city churches or organizations.
- Feeding the homeless in a park while doing street evangelism with those being ministered to.

Rural service

- Painting, cleaning, and/or refurbishing churches that do not have the resources to do the work themselves.
- Doing a cleanup project for schools or community organizations.
- Working on an Indian reservation.
- Working for free for farmers who are financially strapped.
- Rebuilding a dilapidated campground, church, or community building.

Foreign service

- Assisting an organization that specializes in building projects—homes, churches, etc.
- Visiting foreign missionaries and helping them teach

English; setting up a local day-care program or any other project that could provide short-term help.
- Running a camp for the local youth or children.

Local service

- Building projects for low-income churches, housing projects, businesses, or schools.
- Cleaning a highway or downtown district.
- Serving in an elderly neighborhood—mowing lawns, washing cars, etc.

Whatever you decide on as your service retreat, it is imperative that you *know the territory* before you take a group of kids there. If you want to lead your own trip, make sure adequate time and energy is spent on planning every aspect, including such things as any cultural information, the tools and equipment needed, the cooking, water, and waste facilities, etc.

There are many well-qualified youth-group missions organizations available to help plan and execute trips. If you have any doubt about your ability to run a service retreat, seek their help. There are many missions organizations and opportunities available, but here are a few I recommend:

Amor Ministries
2500 E. Nutwood Ave., #121A
Fullerton, CA 92631
714-680-6401

Compassion International
P.O. Box 7000
Colorado Springs, CO 80933
800-336-7676

Habitat for Humanity
419 W. Church St.
Americus, GA 31709
912-924-6935

Horizon Educational Associates
(City Ministry in D.C.)
23 Pickering St.
Essex, MA 01929
508-468-6525

Mountain T.O.P.
2704 12th Ave., S
Nashville, TN 37204
615-298-1575

Bancho Agua Viva Ministries
Box 8495
Chula Vista, CA 92012
619-585-8783

Teen Missions, Inc.
Box 1056
Merritt Island, FL 32952
305-453-0350

The Center for Student Missions
P.O. Box 76
San Juan Capistrano, CA 92693
714-546-6194

Jungle Aviation Radio Service (JARS) World Vision
(Simulate an Amazon jungle P.O. Box 0
experience) Pasadena, CA 91109
Box 248 800-444-2522
Waxhaw, NC 28173
704-843-6000

Sample Schedules

ONE DAY "MINI-RETREAT"
(service in a homeless shelter)

6:30   Leave for retreat.

7:00   Arrive and unload supplies and gifts.

7:30   Help serve meals to the homeless residents.

9:00   Clean up facility.

10:30   Break: gather to discuss feelings, fears, pray for each other.

11:00   Continue cleaning facility.

11:30   Help prepare and serve lunch.

1:30   Clean up from lunch.

2:00   Hit the streets in teams of four (each with a leader) to invite people to a service at the shelter at 4:00.

4:00   Service: mostly singing and testimonies.

5:00   Talk with people who come.

6:00   Serve meals.

8:00   Clean up.

8:30   Depart for home.

WEEKEND TRIP TO SERVE
AN INNER-CITY CHURCH
(in partnership with the youth from
the inner-city church)

Friday

7:00   Leave for church.

7:30   Arrive and unpack.

8:00   Meet with the inner-city church's youth:

singing, mixers, skits, testimonies, message by an inner-city pastor.

10:00	Time of small-group sharing between the two groups of kids.
10:30	Fun, singing, and games.
11:30	Lights out (sleep in church or community hall).

Saturday

7:00	Staff and counselors meet to pray and plan.
7:30	Wake up kids, leaders make breakfast.
8:00	Breakfast in the church, served by the leaders.
8:30	Leaders clean up.
9:00	Work on cleaning and fixing up church.
12:00	Lunch: pizza.
1:00	Go to a park and play games.
2:00	Back to the church to work.
5:00	Prepare for evening program.
6:00	Dinner: guest students cook, serve, and clean up.
7:30	Meeting: singing, sharing, and worshipping together.
9:00	Talent show.
10:30	Casual fellowship and snacks.
11:30	Lights out.

Sunday

7:00	Staff and counselors meet to pray and plan.
7:30	Host kids cook, serve, and clean up.
9:00	Everyone attends worship service together.
11:30	Return home.

WEEK-LONG TRIP
(work with a missions organization
in a Mexican village to complete an orphanage)

Day 1

4:00 A.M.   Leave to arrive that afternoon.

5:00   Arrive in camp, unload gear, set up, make dinner.

7:00   Dinner.

8:30   Brief meeting to meet missionaries and get briefed on work, some singing, Scripture, and prayer.

10:00   Lights out.

Daily Schedule

7:00   Wake up, fix breakfast.

8:00   Quiet time, make lunches.

9:00   Drive to village and work.

12:00   Break for lunch.

1:00   Work.

5:00   Return to camp, rest, and prepare dinner.

6:30   Dinner.

8:00   Fellowship: singing, sharing, message, and prayer.

10:30   Lights out. ◆

... ◆ 13

Planning

Some of the more exciting moments I have had in camping have been during our annual planning retreats. Almost every year of my involvement in youth work has been highlighted by a leadership retreat that had the primary purpose of planning our year (or semester). When we have tried to have a several-hour planning time in someone's living room, either with or without our leadership students, we never seem to make any headway. But just by driving an hour or so away from the everyday routine, our group seems to draw closer together. We are more energetic, more fun, more willing to "waste time" together, and far more creative. Some of the very best and most innovative ideas have come out of planning retreats.

With leadership kids in the mix, the result is even better—they have an opportunity to give some extended thought to what they would like to see happen in the group as well as feel a unity of purpose with the adult leaders. When thoroughly planned and well directed, planning retreats can be the best and most productive retreats you'll have.

Description

A planning retreat is a time when the leadership team (either with or without student leaders) can plan a specific number of events or an activity calendar for a semester or for a year. When students are involved, the retreat must serve a dual purpose; while it is ultimately designed to carry out the business of planning a group's schedule, thought must be taken as to how it can also meet a specific need that the kids attending have. With this in mind, retreats as well as kids need pre-planning, and the same three-step process that all other retreats go through should be followed—developing a vision, setting goals, and deciding on action steps or options to be used.

There are some very valid concerns regarding the use of student leaders as we enter the 1990s. There are those who feel that the sharper, more social type of kids are usually the leaders in Christian youth programs, and yet they are already the leaders in the adolescent community. What this style of programming does, goes the argument, is to reinforce to "out-of-it" kids, the not-so-leadership ones, that they are losers and will remain so, even in the church.

But, on the other hand, the appointment of student leaders, when done with sensitivity, care, and understanding, can be a wonderful gift to young people who desire to grow in their faith, to serve the youth group and the church at large, and who are willing to commit to a certain amount of time and effort. When this becomes a limited criteria for student leadership, a student-leadership group philosophy is a tremendous tool with which to provide opportunities to serve for kids who might not have the same chance in their secular environment.

Purpose

To instill in student leaders a sense of ownership. The best way to motivate any group of people, however enthusiastic, is to instill in them a sense of responsibility and an obligation to the group. When the chips are down, those who feel a sense of ownership are the ones who will step to the front. Without that, many students will be excited until the task gets difficult, cumbersome, or boring.

Goals

- To give students specific guidelines concerning the tasks for which they are responsible. Allowing them to actually own and run the Sunday school program, for example, or every social activity from start to finish, is a good way to help kids see that they are valuable and necessary. The adult staff should set parameters within which the students can work and maintain veto power over any decision that crosses those boundaries. But—and here is the important thing to keep in mind—in attempting to encourage students to own a camping program, once they have made a decision that clearly falls within their realm of responsibility, let them go with it. You may believe in your heart of hearts that it is a bust and will fail miserably, but it is best to let the students learn that for themselves.

- To assign homework prior to the retreat that will force kids to think through their opinions and programming ideas before their arrival. This will help them take the task of planning seriously and realize that their contributions are important.
- To begin the planning process in small groups in which every leader and kid in the small group has an equal voice. Each of these small groups should be given a specific task area to plan, one that is not too large.
- To continue student relationships with adult leaders after the retreat is over. When decisions have been made and responsibilities assigned, continue to have the students meet with and report to their adult leaders. This will help the kids feel trusted and that they have legitimate ideas.

Purpose

To plan group programs in a nonstructured environment. Obviously, a planning retreat is primarily designed for planning a period of time on the calendar. The planning, however, should not be limited to placing the same old format on a calendar and then playing "fill in the blanks." The reason for a non-structured environment is to analyze the group's present condition, foster its creativity, and take steps to improve it. As students and leaders come together with no other agenda than to plan a short term of programs, they will be freed up to think and interact far better than they would at home.

But that is not to say there should be *no* agenda, for sometimes planned informality is necessary to keep a group focussed. During the retreat the mix of personalities may produce the right spark to maintain the energy, but often large amounts of free time set aside for "informal creativity" turn into a nightmare of boredom. More often than not, groups undertaking unstructured retreats discover that creativity rarely happens on its own; there must be some sort of leadership to ensure good use of time.

Goals

- To have the adult team assume the responsibility for filling dead time. They should be prepared to fill gaps with interactive exercises, games, or programs in case the group needs a boost during an afternoon break or in the late evening.
- To gather a few times to sing, laugh, share, and pray as a body. These occasionally flow naturally out of the group's dynamics, and it is wonderful when this happens, but usually planning regular meeting times is a must.
- To have "in the bag" some semblance of a schedule that will keep the group on track to move ahead. Such things as meal times, meeting times, and lights-out times should be very flexible, but the hours for work, play, and interaction should not be left to chance or valuable time may be wasted.

Purpose

To build a deeper commitment to Christ. It makes no sense to ever go on a Christian retreat and neglect this purpose. For most retreats and camps, you may think this would be obvious, but when it comes down to the task-oriented retreats, it is far too easy to get right down to business and neglect the one for whom the gathering was called in the first place! Every time a group of Christians comes together to do "Kingdom" business, we must remember to be people of God before we do the work of God.

Goals

- To begin the planning process with a talk or discussion on the theology of planning. This will help students understand how the Lord fits into our goal-setting and plan-making. You might have students think about whether Christian activities should be planned or allowed to develop spontaneously and then come prepared with their own list of "pros and cons of planning." These lists will help stimulate discussion. It is difficult for Christian adults to comprehend the relationship between prayer and planning, so we must not assume that kids will understand it.

- To open every group gathering with worship singing.
- To spend ample time in prayer before each gathering and brainstorming session, always prior to the formulation of final plans.

Options

As long as the group can sleep, eat, pray, think, and play together as a unified family, a planning retreat can take place almost anywhere. A cabin in the woods, a beach trip, a barn in the middle of nowhere—the location really doesn't matter. The key factor is *time*—enough time away from the ordinary to give people freedom to stop, think, and pray creatively.

It is rarely productive to have planning retreats last longer than three days, and a weekend works best. After two or three days the plans are pretty well defined and the "real work" needs to begin, and that goes beyond the purpose of a planning retreat. On the other hand, you'll need the retreat to last at least overnight and preferably for a twenty-four-hour block of time. This will give the group some time to connect, pray, dream, and organize, all of which are necessities of a planning retreat.

Sample Schedule

WEEKEND PLANNING RETREAT

Friday

5:00	Leave for retreat (eat dinner on the way as a group or wait until you arrive to eat).
8:00	Arrive, get settled.
8:30	Gather to sing, present the purpose of the retreat, and discuss a "theology of Christian planning."
10:00	Group activity (fun).
10:45	Snack.

11:15	Saunter to bed (lights out no later than 12:30; leaders should be last ones to bed).

Saturday

7:30	Gather and pray for weekend (optional).
8:30	Breakfast.
9:30	Break up into small groups to begin brainstorming program tasks.
11:00	Gather to report findings and make recommendations to the group at large.
12:00	Lunch.
1:00	Free time (planned game or activity, if necessary).
3:00	Small groups: take recommendations and develop specific goals and action plans.
5:00	Free time.
6:00	Dinner.
7:30	Gather to sing, share, worship, and pray for planning process.
9:30	Group activity (or let it stay loose if it fits the group).
11:30	Lights out.

Sunday

7:30	Prayer time (optional).
8:30	Breakfast.
9:30	Gather to lay out final goals and action plans for entire program and assign task responsibilities.
12:00	Leave (lunch on the way home). ◆

SECTION THREE

APPENDICES

APPENDIX **A**

A Resource Guide for Camp Counselors

Stan Beard
Director of Ministry Resources
Young Life

Counseling kids at camp is perhaps the most important ministry there is. Sharing life with kids on a twenty-four-hour basis is demanding, draining, and frustrating, but also highly rewarding. Counselors proclaim, clarify, embody, and make real the claims of Christ. Seeing a person live the Christian life is infinitely more convincing than simply hearing someone talk about it. Camp counselors are central to the proclamation process. They make the truths of the Gospel real and personal. Kids see in their counselors the possibility and validity of a life committed to Christ.

The purpose of *A Resource Guide For Outreach Camp Counselors* is to give each person involved in the camp counseling process some basic tools to help in the task. This course alone is not sufficient.

Training sessions in specific areas are necessary to prepare people to be effective counselors. Adults do not have to be highly skilled or professionally trained to be excellent camp counselors. God has equipped many of us to do an outstanding job of loving kids and leading them to Christ. Solid preparation, a life devoted to Christ, and a sincere love for kids are the basic essentials needed.

This manual, we trust, will provide you with the fundamentals in your preparation process.

The Importance of Counseling

1. *Counselors make the message of Christ personal.* We live in an impersonal world. People are crying out for identity—for someone to *know* them and *care* enough to pray for them intelligently. Since we have become a faceless society, it is important to note, in contrast, that Jesus sees everyone in a crowd. *Everyone* is important. We are to follow Christ's example in our camping ministry. Above all, we must be "people centered." Facilities and programs are certainly an integral part, but the *key*, the focal point, must always be *qualified, vital, loving* counselors! This will become increasingly important as society becomes more dehumanized.

2. *Counselors are the "key" to an effective camp.* Most kids will be impressed by the quality of the camp program and the beauty of the property. But the lasting impact of the Gospel on their lives usually comes from the example of their counselor. Counselors and their kids have seven days of *creative* living together to demonstrate the love and personal concern of Christ. As the Scripture states, the counselor is standing "in the place of Christ." They are personal ambassadors, personal representatives of the King of kings and the Lord of lords. This is not a job! It is a strategic mission—and there is quite a difference.

3. *Counselors help clarify the truths of God.* In view of the fact that whole generations have grown up in a society that believes there is no such thing as truth and that everything is relative, it is imperative that trained, loving

counselors be on hand with the knowledge and ability to help these kids see the reality and love of God. There has never been a time in history when skillful, dedicated counselors have been so desperately needed. Patient listening, careful questioning, and personal direction are areas in which counselors can be extremely helpful to kids searching for truth.

4. *Counselors participate in the redemptive process.* The astounding reality of the evangelization process is that God invites us to participate with him in changing lives! What a sacred task! What a unique and priceless privilege. God performs the miracle of new life in each kid's heart, but includes us. We do not "produce" the kingdom of God. We are not ultimately responsible for the work of the Holy Spirit, but he always chooses people as the vehicle through which he works!

    Counseling provides one of the greatest opportunities to help kids see the *total picture* of the Good News of Christ. You will usually have six full days to help them put together the beautiful story of God's love. As the week progresses, they will hear about Christ (who he is), themselves (condition of humanity), the Cross (why Christ died), how to become a Christian, and you will be right in the middle of it with them. It may be your experience to observe the power of the Holy Spirit as he changes lives right before your eyes. There is no greater privilege than being involved as an intimate partner in the redemptive process and seeing God change lives. It's where the action is!

Qualifications for Counselors

1. *Genuine love of Christ.* "For Christ's love compels us . . ." (2 Cor. 5:14). No other motivation is sufficient to carry you through the rigors of working with these kids over a long period of time; Christ's "agape" love just gives and gives and gives without expecting a response.
2. *Sincere love for kids.* "Love must be sincere" (Rom.

12:9). Not everyone can tolerate adolescents! If you are uncomfortable with their music, language, and style of life, it could be an indication you will have difficulty relating to them. Do not fake it—they can spot a phony a mile off.

3. *Flexibility and the ability to hang loose.* "Preach the Word; be prepared in season and out of season; correct, rebuke and encourage—with great patience and careful instruction" (2 Tim. 4:2). This, of course, does not mean you do not have a plan or purpose and direction in your counseling. It just means that you will be involved in unstructured situations. Each day and each week brings a different set of circumstances. If you can't flex, you will be totally frustrated.

4. *Enthusiasm.* "Whatever you do, work at it with all your heart, as working for the Lord, not for men" (Col. 3:23). Gloom and negativism is contagious—so is enthusiasm! You must encourage campers in everything: food, speakers, accommodations, programs, and of course, the Lord. Ask questions positively! Get campers in the habit of saying "yes" and you will be surprised how catching this attitude is.

5. *Loyalty.* "All men will know that you are my disciples if you love one another" (John 13:35). If the leadership team (the body of Christ) functions in harmony and genuine love, evangelism takes place as a logical result. This means that we support one another, empathize with one another, and encourage one another. We esteem others better than ourselves. If someone on the leadership team makes an apparent error in judgment, does something you feel is wrong, or says something with which you disagree, it is still your responsibility to support that person. The right thing to do is to go to the one in charge and state your case. Individuality plus conformity equals harmony, which results in community! The body of Christ in action is God's primary way of communication.

6. *Dependability.* "Rather, we have renounced secret and shameful ways; we do not use deception, nor do we

distort the word of God . . ." (2 Cor. 4:2). The greatest ability is dependability! If you fulfill all your responsibilities to the best of your ability, you will see a camp that clicks and is effective.

7. *Confidentiality.* "Be very careful, then how you live—not as unwise but as wise" (Eph. 5:15). It is imperative that we keep personal information confidential. If a young person confides in us, we are duty bound to share the matter with no one, except the head counselor if his/her counsel is needed. In certain extreme cases of abuse, violence, etc., we are legally required to report what we hear. The head counselors should definitely be involved if this kind of situation comes up.

8. *Strength and firmness.* "Be strong in the Lord and in his mighty power" (Eph. 6:10). Remember that you are a son or daughter of the King of kings and the Lord of lords with all the rights and privileges that go with it. Therefore act like one, in royal humility. Most kids will respond to strong, consistent leadership. Respect and friendship is usually strengthened, not lost, with a counselor who firmly leads a kid or a cabin time.

9. *Cheerfulness.* "Rejoice in the Lord always . . ." (Phil. 4:4). A good sense of humor will get you through many difficult circumstances and add to the enjoyment of all. Kids need to laugh. They need to be around positive, upbeat people. They will feel welcome in an atmosphere of love and laughter. The constant reminder of what Christ has done and is continuing to do for us should always cause us to rejoice.

10. *Sensitivity.* "Each of you should look not only to your own interests, but also to the interests of others. Your attitude should be the same as that of Christ Jesus" (Phil. 2:4–5). Compassion is feeling the need of others to the point that you do something about it. Biblical love is not passive; it is always active. It reaches out. It emphasizes. It is personal. Ask yourself, what would Christ do? Be very tender with kids' feelings. They need to be treated with compassion.

11. *Patience.* "Be joyful in hope, patient in affliction, faithful in prayer" (Rom. 12:12). To be in a cabin with teenagers is not easy. We tend to be judges when we should be patient friends. The Lord is patient with us. Many of the most important spiritual breakthroughs happen with kids long after the week at camp is over. Patience will keep you from expecting too much too soon.

12. *Consistency of spiritual life.* "I am the vine; you are the branches. If a man remains in me and I in him, he will bear much fruit; apart from me you can do nothing" (John 15:5). "Do not be anxious about anything, but in everything, by prayer and petition, with thanksgiving, present your requests to God" (Phil. 4:6). There is no way to be an effective counselor apart from a daily vital personal walk with Christ. Make time for prayer and Bible reading. Seek out someone with whom you can share your discoveries.

Counselor Responsibilities

1. To Other Camp Personnel
   a. *Head Counselor*—Bring any problem to the head counselor. It is his or her responsibility to help you in any counseling matter. Sometime during each day you are to report to him/her concerning your campers' reactions, both positive and negative, to messages, group meetings, programs, and your own personal feelings. The head counselor will pass the information on to the camp manager and other necessary personnel.

   Counselor's meetings should not be used for reporting reactions. They should be times for sharing Christ and our lives together. Head counselors will work out the time and place for daily reporting.
   b. *Program Director*—Enter into the program suggestions with gusto. Support the director by seeing to it that your campers are there on time and in the middle of all the action. Pray for her/him.
   c. *Camp Manager*—Whatever they say goes! They are

in charge. Once a decision is made, support it with enthusiasm. Pray for the ability to make the message clear. Encourage your campers to interact with the camp manager. Demonstrate that you support the manager and lead your kids to do the same.

d. *Other Counselors*—"Be wise in the way you act toward outsiders; make the most of every opportunity" (Col. 4:5). Keep in mind that we are engaged in a spiritual conflict. Most of your time should be given enthusiastically to your campers. *We are not there for each other*. This is not the time or place to "make points" with the opposite sex. Certainly we should take a small portion of time to share our lives with each other. However, your campers are a sacred trust, and time that can be spent with them should be carefully guarded.

There will be time in between camps to soak up fellowship and get to know one another.

Ask God to give you love and respect for your fellow counselors. Our attitudes and actions toward each other will communicate more clearly than anything else.

e. *Work Crew*—These dedicated young people are responsible for many of the physical tasks necessary to the operation of the camp. They are directly responsible to the work crew bosses.

It will be your privilege to respect them, introduce them to your campers, encourage dialogue between them and your kids. With the work crew bosses' permission, invite one or two into your cabin. Have them share their lives with the campers. With your guidance, the work crew kids will have a powerful impact on campers.

You must understand that *work crew kids* should not become involved romantically or as friends with counselors. Their job is a big one and they need to focus on serving the camp.

f. *Counseling Process*—Generally speaking, it is appropriate for males to counsel males and females to counsel females. When exceptional situations occur, check out the appropriateness of "opposite sex" counseling with either the head counselors or an experienced staff person at camp. Use sensitivity and caution in this area.

   g. *Christians in Your Cabin*—Outreach camps aim to make the claims of Christ understandable to non-Christians and are not set up for nurture and spiritual growth.

Because of this it is suggested that the counselor meet regularly with any Christian kid or kids to encourage spiritual growth. It is the head counselor's responsibility to provide campaigner-type sessions for the Christian kids in camp. Christian kids can be valuable assets in a camp situation in the areas of prayer, friendship, and example. Encourage them to not dominate cabin discussions with "right" answers.

2. To Your Campers

   a. Learn their names quickly. Introduce yourself to them as their counselor and make them feel welcome. From the start, friendliness and enthusiasm count.

   b. You will have the sole responsibility of those assigned to you. See that they enjoy camp and that they enter into the activities of the camp. Their good time may depend on your ability to get them involved in all the activities and on your enthusiasm for each activity.

   c. Discipline

- *See that your campers attend all the meetings and activities.* Quickly check and see that they are present. If not, find them and get them to participate. Get the head counselors to help you locate the kids if necessary.

- *Enforce lights out rule in your cabin.* When a certain time is given to be quiet, cooperate by seeing that your campers are in their quarters and lights are out. This will have its effect on other cabins if lights are not out on time. The kids need their rest.

Clean up is usually done each morning. It is the counselor's responsibility to see that the jobs are assigned and performed to meet the individual camp requirements. (This does not mean that you have to do all the work, but see that it is done).

- *Be positive and consistent in your disciplinary actions.* This will help you gain the respect of your campers.
- *Do not hand out punishments indiscriminately, and once you commit yourself, keep your word regarding punishment.*

d. You will have the responsibility of leading them in their discussion time at night.

e. You must seek to lead them concerning matters of the Lord, not only in the discussions at night, but when you are with them during the week. Most of the time the initiative must be taken by the counselor in such a conversation. Short, quality cabin discussions are usually better than long, drawn out ones.

f. General responsibilities

- *Know where your kids are at all times.* You are responsible for them. You are the camp director for your kids. We want them to be at all activities, meetings, and meals.
- *Do not allow kids to cut meals or meetings* unless they see the head counselor, nurse, or doctor. Encourage them to get their "money's worth" and experience the entire camp.
- *Kids are not to leave camp* unless they first check with the camp manager.
- *Do not tell kids the whole schedule ahead of time.* Let the program director unfold each new day. Anticipation and discovery are half the fun.
- *Do not let kids see notes, information, or schedules that are passed out to counselors.*

3. To Your Own Spiritual Life

a. Make time to be alone with the Lord each day. True, camp is strenuous! That is all the more reason for spiritual resources.

b. Seek out someone with whom you can spontaneously share your life! Someone who naturally lifts you to the Lord. Schedule time to share with them your joys and concerns.

c. Expect God to teach you and surprise you with his goodness. You are not ultimately responsible for your kids response to the Gospel. Enjoy loving them and look for God to reveal himself to you as well as to them.

Camp Preparation

Good preparation begins long before kids get on the bus. Here are several things for counselors to consider prior to camp.

1. *The importance of prayer.* Enlist a number of Christians in your community to pray for you and your kids daily. Remember to report back to them after the camp experience is over. They will be interested in how God has touched lives.

2. *Information for parents.* Give parents and/or guardians sufficient information about the details and logistics of the trip. Parents'/guardians' meetings, camp newsletters, phone calls, etc. are all very helpful to parents. Teenagers usually do not communicate all the specifics of a trip to their parents. Good, complete information from your staff or counselors will build a great deal of trust and confidence.

3. *Physical, emotional, and spiritual preparation.* Effective counselors will get ample sleep prior to the trip. Beginning a counseling experience tired and worn out is a bad way to start. Leave the pressures of home behind. Bringing homework or unfinished projects and making business phone calls and decisions while at camp are distractions. Clean the slate as much as possible to give one hundred percent to the counseling responsibility. A week of camp counseling takes total effort! The challenge is overwhelming, but the outcome is worth it! Come ready to counsel.

Camp Program

The classic outreach camp program is designed to help counselors relate to kids and to create an environment in which campers and their counselors may consider the claims of Christ together. Everything during the week should help counselors build friendships and encourage evangelism. The program is the vehicle that gets the camper involved to the extent that he/she will be ready to consider carefully the truths of the Gospel.

Program

Event	Purpose	Counselor Responsibility
Bus/Van Trip	Safe arrival at camp	1. Learn names; get to know kids. 2. Set stage; get kids ready for the big week. 3. Good, relaxed, but firm supervision.
Arrival at camp		1. Cabin assignments and location. 2. Meet head counselor and know where first counselor meeting will be. 3. Help kids with luggage.
First evening	Setting the stage for kids to feel welcome, included, and safe.	1. Sit with kids at first meal. 2. Encourage program participation. 3. Build unity and spirit in cabin.

Typical Camp Day

7:30   Wake up.
- Make sure kids get up!
- Provide time for personal spiritual growth.

8:30   Breakfast.
- One counselor per table/socialize.

9:30–10:30   Group meetings (to get kids to think about important things of life).

- See that all campers attend.
- Share in ministry of leader by prayer.
- Don't get "shaken" if kids react violently to discussion leader.

10:30–12:30 Free time (swimming, horseback riding, volleyball, basketball).
- Stay with the kids; be winning their confidence.

12:30 Lunch.

1:30–5:00 Free time.
- Encourage creative use of free time. Do things with kids.

5:30 Counselor-in-training.
- Training period for junior counselors in counseling skills.

6:30 Dinner.

7:15 Counselors' meeting (pulse of camp and prayer).
- Provide information on campers to group and speakers.
- Sharing our lives as the body of Christ.
- Prayer.

8:30–9:30 Club meeting.
- Hustle kids to meeting. Sit with them.
- Pray for your kids during club.

9:30–10:30 Cabin time (discussion with kids).
- Lead the discussion.
- Ask good questions.
- Let them do most of the talking.

10:30–11:30 Program events (games, entertainment, etc.).

12:30 Lights out.
- Enforce this little custom of sleep. Strong leadership is often needed at this point.

Counseling Situations

Friendships with Kids

This important part of counseling must not be under-emphasized or the effectiveness of solid counseling will be undermined. No camper will open up to a counselor who has not taken the time to be a friend; to do so is to win the right to be heard, for we will always value the advice of a friend.

Ways to build genuine friendships:

1. *Be a good listener.* Find out the interests of the various campers and do what you can to promote their interests. Ask good questions that show you are really interested in their lives.
2. *Be available.* Let the campers know that you are looking forward to being with them for the week. This availability is best shown in attitude, not mere words. Set specific times to swim, play basketball, hike, etc. with your kids.
3. *Bear with campers' idiosyncracies.* Sometimes it is easy for us adults to look "down our noses" at some of the attitudes and interests of the kids. This will hinder our ministry with them.
4. *Exercise tough love.* Kids want to look at you as their leader. They expect you to act like a leader and not like one of the gang. This is sometimes hard for young leaders.
5. *Be positive.* When you live before these kids, let the love of the Lord Jesus shine brightly through you. A spirit of cheerfulness is so important.
6. *Be yourself.* Do not try to copy another's personality. Let the Holy Spirit individually direct your abilities as you present the Savior. You are uniquely gifted and qualified to love the kids in your cabin.

Opportunities for Counseling

Several opportunities for discussion will be structured during the camp experience. These are not times for messages or lectures, but for discussions designed to allow the counselee to crystalize and modify his/her thinking and feelings. Initially, it will be important for you, the counselor, to create an atmosphere of openness and to establish trust. During this phase you should work at understanding your counselees, showing them warmth and acceptance and being a real person yourself. In light of this, you must make sure that you listen and understand clearly what each counselee is saying. You must also show unconditional respect for individuals even though their behavior might be questionable, and you must share openly your own thoughts and feelings.

1. *Cabin times.* Since you will probably be living in a cabin with several high-school campers, you have a natural setting for dialogue. It is assumed that the camping experience for you as a counselor begins with the trip to camp and that you have used this time to get to know kids and to let them know you. Thus, an atmosphere of openness and trust is already in its early stages of development as you arrive at camp. It would seem important to devote your first time together as a cabin to get to know each other. This is especially important for those individuals who did not travel to camp together. During this time counselors can make a few personal observations and thereby show an interest in each person and help to relax the group. Though these comments or observations can be of a humorous nature, genuine interest might be demonstrated more quickly by asking clarifying questions or by noting significant experiences. This will probably be your first structured opportunity for discussion, and it will be an important time for developing a trusting atmosphere.

These "cabin times" throughout the week will provide structure for your kids to reflect on the day's activities. During the early phases of camp you might use leading questions to help your group get started. At first these questions should be general to allow your kids the freedom to respond as they feel. Such questions as, "How is camp going for you?" or "How have you responded to what has gone on so far?" would be appropriate. A good counselor learns to listen intently to the responses of the counselees and works hard at clarifying vagueness, commenting on personal situations, and expressing real emotions of joy, concern, sadness, etc. in response to what is being said. Here are some thoughts on listening.

a. Repeat what you hear the person saying to be sure you understand him/her. For example, "Do I hear you saying that you . . ." In this way you clear up misconceptions and learn to read your counselee more accurately.

b. Restate a question to clarify the meaning. Example: "How do you know there is a God?" Rephrase: "What evidence might you give to indicate there is a God?" "What struck you about what _____ said in the talk about the existence of God?" Always be aware of the possibility that your question might be relevant only to you, or that your group needs time to formulate their thoughts. Hopefully an open atmosphere will allow and encourage the group to express any feelings about irrelevancy, and your own anxiety level will allow you to remain at ease while they think. You might even suggest some answers, but above all be sure that you are reading their needs and feelings accurately and are asking questions accordingly.

c. Be specific when you ask questions during cabin discussion. General, vague questions directed at the group are not as effective as asking individuals within the group. Example: "John, what were you feeling when the speaker mentioned _____"?

Resentment, hostility, or other such attitudes that arise during the discussion might be best dealt with on an individual basis at another time. It is too easy for a counselor to use the group against one person who is antagonistic rather than to give that person the opportunity to work through his/her feelings. The counselor's resentment, hostility, or guilt might also be best handled at another time with the head counselor. The primary purpose of the discussion is to give the counselees an opportunity to express their own lifestyles within the context of the Christian message. Though summing up a discussion time is not necessarily important, it would seem important for a counselor in this type of setting to make mental notes of where individual counselees are. This will be valuable for the counselor when talking with counselees individually. Also, if some particularly important things happened during the session, a brief summary might help clarify those things that are relevant.

If you plan to make the evening time before bed a regular cabin discussion, inform your kids on the first night that this will be occuring and encourage them to be informal and relaxed. If you mention that it will be a short time each night, stick to that. Your credibility reflects your respect for them.

2. *Small group discussions.* In addition to the living-group discussion there will probably be other opportunities for structured discussion following role plays, message meetings, or during special meetings. If you are leading one of these discussions groups, an atmosphere of understanding, regard, and genuineness must still be established for good communication to take place. Thus, leaders must work hard at listening. Although these discussions will be less intense and personal than your living-group discussions, they do help communicate the total picture of the Gospel.

Helping Kids Begin to Follow Christ

The sacred opportunity for counselors in many cases will be to help a teenager take that first step toward saying yes to Jesus Christ. Ultimately, this is a divine transaction between the Holy Spirit and the camper. To over-counsel at this point would be a mistake. Effective counselors know how to assist kids to begin their walk with Christ, but will not try to control the words, emotions, and responses. God has been building his family since the dawn of human history, using various methods, styles, and people. None of us has a "corner on truth" when it comes to leading someone to Christ.

Below are some guidelines to consider:

1. *Help kids comprehend the centrality of Christ in the salvation process.* Help them understand that the birth, life, death, and resurrection of Christ is real and personal. He came, lived, died, and rose for them! Use stories and verses from the Scriptures to underscore the importance of Christ. Colossians 1:15–20, Philippians 2:5–12.
2. *Allow kids to grapple with the reality and severity of the problem of sin.* Help them see how wide is the gap and vast is the division between God and people not united by Christ. Emphasize relational separation from God more than personal "behavioral mistakes." Being lost (far) from God is more devastating than being "bad." Both, of course, are sin, but God fundamentally wants to restore broken relationships, not simply improve behavior.

   Kids need to know how lost they are before they will appreciate how loved they are. Scriptural texts in Romans 1–3 and 7, Ephesians 2, Colossians 1:21–23, and the Gospels emphasize this truth.
3. *Encourage the process of salvation more than the experience.* Quite often, overzealous counselors will press kids to feel something, say something, or do something to make sure the kid can point to a conscious moment, feeling, or place that will validate the exact time when God entered his or her life. Though the intention of this type of counseling is usually noble, it has the tendency to reduce the mystery and sacredness of how God is working in a person's heart.

   Long before camp, God has been bringing people, experiences, attitudes, and questions into kids' lives, shaping them to respond to him. And long after the camp is over, God will continue to love, lead, and mold the lives of those kids. We are privileged to participate in the process, but we are not responsibile for producing the experience!

   Allow kids to feel, question, and doubt. Encourage them to move at their own pace. Challenge them to entrust their lives into Christ's care, but do not rely on a particular formula to make it happen. God's spirit is quite capable of drawing kids to himself.

Encourage kids to spend time alone in quiet reflection. Ask them hard and challenging questions about Christ and spiritual things. Help them to know the implications of being a follower of Christ. But do not tell them *exactly* how to become a Christian or try to explain to them how to feel. We simply do not fully know (see Eph. 1:3–14).

4. *Emphasize that God's commitment to them is stronger than their initial commitment to God.* Kids need to know and feel confident that God, not them, is really the author and creator of the salvation process. It is God's good decision about them that takes precedence over a kid's decision about God. Yes, the relationship is mutual, but kids need to know that God is actively working to draw them close to his heart, and that he will not run away if a kid stumbles, falls, doubts, sins, etc. Romans 8 and John 17 are good places to direct kids in this issue.

5. *Encourage kids to see beginning with Christ as the start of a long and vast journey.* They need to know that maturity and development will be gradual. Birth is important, but it is only a starting point.

Many factors will contribute to strengthening one's relationship with Christ. Below are some aspects of the journey of faith.

a. *The importance of church* (the larger body of Christ). Help young Christians get started in some form of regular worship in their local community. Introduce them to people who could assist them in building an active and consistent love of worship and service.

b. *The necessity of Scripture.* Point kids toward effective ways to make the Bible and its truths a regular part of their Christian growth. Personal reading, Bible study groups, verse memory, and personal discipleship are some of the ways to help make Scripture central for kids.

c. *The joy of Scripture.* Very early in the faith journey of a young Christian, the challenge of service should be taught. The body of Christ is a giving, sharing, and serving body. There are numerous ways to help kids begin to serve, but let them know that life in Christ will mean working with him in his world.

d. *The privilege and purpose of prayer.* Teach young Christians to pray! Let them know how vital a regular communication link with God is. Make sure they learn that prayer is more than figuring out our wants and needs and then putting together a request list. Teach them the joy and necessity of regular intimate communion with God.

e. *The membership responsibilities in the Christian family.* Faith in Christ, though personal, is not an experience. Fellowship, learning, and sharing our lives in Christ is a corporate experience. Provide environments or help kids find groups in which authenticity, vulnerability, compassion, and commitment are expressed between group members. Kids need Christian communities to grow and stay healthy.

The Basics of the Gospel

Helping Kids Understand
the Road to Commitment
and the Need for Redemption

THEME	SCRIPTURE	PURPOSE/TRUTH
Creation	Genesis 13, Psalm 8	God's universe and God's people were specially created by and for a loving, caring creator.
Fall (sin)	Romans 13 and 7, Genesis 3	God's human creation turned away to live separate from the creator. Humankind decided to live without a relationship with God. All people, being sinful, are in need of God's restoration.

THEME	SCRIPTURE	PURPOSE/TRUTH
Christr	Matthew, Mark, Luke, John, Colossians 1:15–21, Philippians 2:5–12	God, expressing himself in human terms through his son, Jesus Christ, came to reveal God and also pay the price for sin and separation from God.
Cross/ Resurrection	Matthew 27–28 Mark 15–16 Luke 23–25 John 19–20	God, in Christ, gave his life on the cross as sufficient sacrifice for the sins of the world. God raised Christ through the resurrection to rule and to reign eternally as head of the new creation of all who trust and follow him.
Response to Christ's call to his Kingdom	John 3:1–21, Ephesians 2:8–10, 2 Corinthians 5:17–21, Ephesians 2:19–22	God's spirit calls people to trust in Christ, to turn away from the old life of sin and separation, and follow him. The spirit of God comes to dwell in each person's life, empowering him or her to live for Christ and to be a member of his family.
Christian Life and Responsibility	Colossians 3:1–17, Ephesians 4–6, Matthew 25:31–46	God calls his family to a life of truth, service, and justice. Christians are responsible to live lives worthy of his call and be faithful to his word.
Future/ Eternity/ Return of Christ	Revelation 20–22 Matthew 24–25	Christ will return to earth and establish his kingdom, and all who have trusted and followed him will live and serve forever with him.

Role of a Leader at Camp with Kids from Troubled Families

1. Familiarize yourself with the family background of kids in your cabin. Ask them questions like: "What was it like to grow up in your family?" "Tell me about your parents'

relationship. How do you get along with your mom/ dad?" "Describe your relationship with your siblings," etc.

2. There are three main unwritten rules in a family in which there has been alcoholism and/or abuse:

"Don't talk."
"Don't trust."
"Don't feel."

So you may have a hard time getting kids from these kinds of situations to open up to you and express themselves. This will be an important signal that something may be wrong. Listed below are some suggestions to help kids get beyond each of these roles (these suggestions will also apply to death and divorce situations):

"Don't talk"

It is important for you to remember that kids mostly need you to draw them out and listen to what is going on with them. Let them "teach you about their lives." This is not a time to give a lot of advice or try to fix it. (Responses such as "tell me more about . . ." will help you to get more information.)

"Don't trust"

Because trust is such an issue, following through with kids, both during and after camp, is especially important. In a family where they probably had no adult to count on consistently, regular contact with you will help build faith that someone is going to be there for them.

"Don't feel"

Encourage expression of feelings: "How did it feel to have a Mom who . . . ?" "Sounds like you were angry . . . , sad . . . , etc." Offering empathetic responses such as "that must really hurt" or "that must have been hard for you" will let them know you are with them.

3. If you have a question about a situation that a kid is

dealing with (especially if it involves abuse of *any* kind), talk with the head counselor or camp manager about it. We sometimes have a tendency to minimize problems that frighten us, so do not always trust your own judgment. Check it out with someone else.

A Word from a Property Manager's Viewpoint

Bruce Kramer
Property Manager
Young Life's Frontier Ranch
Buena Vista, Colorado

F rontier Ranch is located in the most spectacular country on earth! We sit at the foot of Mount Princeton, one of Colorado's famous 14,000-foot peaks, and we are very proud of the facility that God has given us. It is a beautiful place with great amenities—horses, Honda Odyssey's, a huge pool with an incredible water slide, great kitchen and dining facilities, meeting rooms, and warm, spacious dormitories and cabins. We on the staff count ourselves fortunate to work on such a property!

But the reason we love working here has little to do with tremendous facilities or modern equipment. The great joy of serving God at a Christian camp like Frontier Ranch is knowing that we are being used to bring people closer to Jesus Christ. As the groups roll in and out of camp almost every weekend during the school year, the buses unload hundreds of kids each week to hear the Gospel, many for the first time. My wife, Cindy, and I, along with the rest of our staff, never cease to be thankful that we can play a small role in reaching kids.

I say this because over the years I have sensed from many youth leaders that they think we, as property staff, approach camping with different motives and agendas. I believe that nothing could be further from the truth. It is important for any youth camping leader to understand that the reason property people get into Christian camping in the first place is that they are offered the opportunity to play a role in ministry without having the call or gifts to be "on the front lines" with kids. From my experience in Christian camping, nearly every cook, plumber, maintenance man or woman, wrangler, and lifeguard has the same sense of calling and awareness of the urgency for young people to come to know Christ as any direct-ministry youth worker.

With this as a backdrop, let me offer the following eight bits of advice to remember when you deal with a property manager or facility director for any camp or retreat:

1. Treat us as colleagues in ministry, not as people you are forced to do business with. We will respond much better if we feel you are a friend who cares for us and not just a bargain hunter looking for the best deal.

2. Read all correspondence *carefully*, especially the contract, well in advance of the camp. Make sure that any questions or problems are handled up front, with enough lead time to make changes. For the most part, if a property feels that you are willing to take seriously their needs, timing, finances, and staff, they will bend over backward to help you.

3. If at all possible, visit the facility well in advance of your event and make an appointment with someone in charge (either the manager, superintendent, or host for your stay) and walk through the property and schedule. We *love* to talk with you, show you around, and help you in any way possible.

4. Make sure that you clearly spell out what is expected and see if there is anything unwritten that is expected of you. For example, if you want coffee provided before break-

fast for your leaders, tell us before 11:00 P.M. Friday night. (A service like this may include a nominal cost, but the cost will rise significantly with last-minute demands!)

5. During phone calls prior to the camp, give some idea of what you hope to accomplish, how we can pray for you as a staff, etc. Inform us of your hopes and dreams for the kids coming to camp.

6. Once at camp, please take the rules seriously. The greatest struggles and problems we have with those using our facility are in this area. Communicate clear expectations and boundaries to the kids and have your leadership be the enforcers (they, after all, have the relationships, while our staff can seem like "cops"!) on things like smoking areas, showing respect for the property, and off-limits buildings, housing, etc. Those leaders who tell their kids that we are friends who want to serve them, even though there are some necessary rules to follow, tend to have the easiest time with discipline in this area.

7. Make sure the staff and counselors are encouraged to take leadership with kids in how they treat our staff. The rudest people at camp are the leaders, and sometimes even the "professional" staff, who expect to be served like royalty. Sometimes the snack shop line is long and the service is slow, but *please* make sure the adults set an example to kids about what it means to be patient and merciful. Nothing harms the spirit and service of a property camp staff like rude or demanding leaders.

8. Finally, encourage my staff. Many of them are young and insecure, and some aren't even sure of their faith. The best way you can serve me (and the Kingdom!) is to love and serve our people. A friendly word, a moment to show appreciation, a note after a meal to the kitchen staff—these all help to remind our folks that the work we do is necessary and valuable.

Thank you for bringing your kids to us. There is no greater joy than knowing that the work my staff and I do every day—overseeing budgets, fixing toilets, mending broken doors—is providing a means for kids to draw closer to Christ. We really are in this thing together! ◆

APPENDIX C

How to Lead a Discussion

Chap Clark

Taken from *Option Plays* by Chap Clark, Duffy Robbins, and Mike Yaconelli. Copyright © 1990 Youth Specialties, Inc.

While speaking at a ski camp a few years ago, I was asked to set up the cabin time. "The leaders have been trained and are ready to lead the discussions," I was told. "All you have to do is explain what a cabin time is and give the kids their meeting places."

After the groups had formed and begun, I sat in the back of the main meeting room where the guys' groups were gathered and glanced around to see how the discussions were going. I noticed a pattern emerging: For every group discussion, there were five leader monologues. The longer I watched, the more obvious it became that these counselors understood a "discussion" to be an opportunity for them to give another message.

Ears Open and Mouths Closed

Unfortunately, that camp experience is all too typical. We may understand and agree with the necessity for group discussion and interaction; yet, our desire to "preach the word in season and out of season" compels us to keep hammering home our version of the truth. What we fail to realize is that words alone do not change behavior. Kids need to get personally involved with a concept before significant change can occur. And kids need the chance to struggle with new information in order to be convinced that they need the input. While solid biblical content is necessary as the foundation for understanding, time for reflection, analysis, and digestion of any content is just as essential to helping people grow.

This is especially true for today's kids. They are constantly barraged with new information, yet they have fewer and fewer opportunities to express their opinions. Rarely do friends ask questions, and many of the authorities in their lives seem to be more interested in expressing their views than in caring about what anyone else thinks. Discussion is crucial, therefore, because it encourages kids to not only share what they know, but what they feel—a level of sharing many adolescents rarely experience. We in youth ministry owe it to the ones we serve to program opportunities for discussion and interaction. To many kids, this will be the most valuable gift we give them—the permission to think and speak.

But there is more to leading a discussion than being committed to getting kids to talk. We must know and understand what it means to lead without stifling a group. And we must be prepared with solid content that is easy to use.

Once the content is delivered and there is a base from which to work, the hard part begins—getting the students to talk. Leading this type of discussion may come naturally to some, but for most of us it is an art to be developed. On the other hand, almost anyone can be taught to lead a discussion that gives students a sense of value as they learn about and grow in their faith.

Ground Rules for Great Discussion

Effective sharing doesn't just happen. It's a challenge to keep mistrust, domination, elitism, and other relational problems from short-circuiting the group process. The following are some ground rules to keep in mind when called upon to lead any discussion. As we take time and energy to build these tips into our leadership styles, we will develop the skills to make any discussion fun, as well as helpful, for the kids we serve.

Freedom (and Safety) of Speech

Evan never said much in our guys' Bible study group. He only answered those questions directed specifically to him. As the months went on, I had pegged Evan as a quiet kid. That next spring I took Evan and a few other guys (none of whom were in our Bible study) to camp. Was I in for a shock! During the cabin time, it was all I could do to keep Evan from dominating. He talked about his feelings, his family, and his faith. That night I realized that Evan didn't feel safe in our group back home. He had been forced to become shy.

For our discussion groups to be helpful to every student involved, we must be sensitive to our Evans—those kids who have a great deal to offer but, for one reason or another, don't feel free to be themselves. We must create a safe group environment, a place where kids can express their thoughts and feelings without fear of ridicule.

Trust is seldom built where relationships are absent. I had expected Evan to open up to the other guys simply because they were involved in the same youth group and went to the same school. But Evan was in a completely different crowd at school than the others, and, outside of our weekly times, never had any contact with the rest of the group. Once I discovered this, I worked harder at programming opportunities for relationships to develop within the Bible study group—an overnight for "just the guys," a dinner and ball game, impromptu movie nights. In a short time, Evan began to be himself with the group. He knew them, they were his friends, and he felt safe enough to contribute.

Small(ish) Is Beautiful

Opinions vary as to the optimum size for a discussion group. Some say there should be no fewer than four and no more than eight; some go as high as twelve. However, we rarely have the luxury of creating the "perfect" sized group. We may have fourteen students who want to stay together and only one leader who can be committed to them. Or there may only be two or three kids in a group. As much as is possible, we should try to arrange groups of between four and seven kids and one to two leaders.

Mum's the Word

There must be a spoken commitment to confidentiality. If anyone feels that what they say in the group may be used against them—even in jest—it will take deep healing to restore any sense of trust.

There is an implied commitment to confidentiality in most small groups when things get "heavy." But kids can be insensitive and forgetful, and many a youth group has been torn apart by an inappropriate word or uncalled-for sarcasm. This rule should be articulated repeatedly.

Question Time

My roommate in college was one of the all-time great question askers. Dave seldom entered a discussion without first saying, "Let me ask you . . ." And never did he let you get away with a simple yes or no—he always wanted to know what you thought or felt. I guess that's why I liked being around Dave. I felt valuable with him because what I had to say mattered. And he was able to communicate that just by the way he asked questions.

How we ask a question is just as important as *what* we ask. The quickest way to ruin a discussion is to allow "yes/no/I don't know" answers to dominate. The skill is in the phrasing of the question. For example, "Do you think that Sarah was wrong in lying to her parents?" gives too much room for a yes or no. On the other hand, questions like "What alternatives did Sarah have to lying to her parents?" or "Why did Sarah feel she had to lie to her folks?" have a better chance of getting a considered response.

It is also important that we get students to talk about how they *feel* about something as well as what they think. In the above example, the way to get a "feeling" response might be: "If you were Sarah, how would you feel about having to lie to your parents?" or "How would you feel if you were Sarah's father or mother and you found out that she had lied to you?"

Silence Is Golden

The students in my discussion groups have become used to silence. They know it is one of my favorite tools in leading a discussion. For the newcomers who giggle at a five-second lapse, I often explain that I like silence. It helps me to think about what the last person said and gather my thoughts for the next comment.

The obvious danger in silence is that a lull in the discussion might hurt the interaction process. This is where the timing of a skilled leader is essential. We have to know when to let silence hang and when to interject a new thought. This takes practice, and there is no ready-made technique that fits every situation. One rule of thumb: If *we* feel like the present track is a dead end, let's move on! However, if we know that some dead time will give kids time to think and possibly push a quieter kid to respond, we should allow ample time to respond. If we are careful observers, we can often "feel" the difference.

A Little Honest Tension

Tension, either naturally developed or artificially introduced, is healthy for any group discussion. Without an element of struggle, there is no real point in having a discussion. If everyone already feels the same way about an issue or topic, there is no growth or movement. And without growth, a discussion is a pointless academic exercise.

Along with silence, creating a sense of tension or frustration over a certain statement or issue is a great discussion-starting tool. Most kids have been programmed to parrot easy answers to complex issues. But life is not nearly so simple, and the best way to get kids to dig deeper in discussion is to strip away their opportunity to fall back on an "easy" answer.

Developing an Effective Leadership Style

Sue was loving, compassionate, and a loyal friend to kids. She was also strong, opinionated, and rarely allowed room for disagreement. When the fall term began, Sue led a weekly Bible-study group for a dozen senior girls who wanted to grow in their faith. Within a few months, however, the girls stopped coming to the Bible study. All the excuses sounded good, but we soon found out that, due to Sue's controlling style, the girls felt they were not free to share their honest opinions about the issues they faced every day, so they dropped out of the group one by one.

Fred was hip, admired, and well liked. His Bible study reflected the guy's attitudes toward him—they were consistent and loyal. But over the course of six months, there was little growth in the lives of the guys. Most of them dropped out of church and were becoming known as the "Christian partiers." When I visited the group to see what was going on, the problem was obvious. Fred would start with solid input, but would soon allow the guys to ignore the content and justify their attitudes and behavior while Fred just sat back looking on. Fred wanted so much to be liked that he was afraid to call them back to the Bible.

Both of these leadership styles illustrate how who we are profoundly affects how well we are able to lead discussions that will help kids in their walks with Christ. While we do need to be ourselves and lead from who we are, there are three essential qualities for an effective discussion leader:

Build relationships with every member of the group. We are responsible to make sure that every person in the group feels known and cared for. It is up to us to ensure that there is a sense of trust and safety within the group. The place to begin is in our individual relationships with every member of the group. If students know and trust us, they are far more likely to open up in the group.

Try to say something individually to every member of the group, even if it's only a few words, before and after each meeting. Whenever a comment is made during the discussion, we should affirm that student. Things as simple as a pat on the hand, a wink, a nod, or a "thank you" will tell our kids that they are valuable and that what they have to say is important.

Don't be afraid to lead. There is a delicate balance between heavy-handed leadership and allowing a verbal free-for-all. At some point, we must make sure that the group is aware of what the Bible has to say on a given issue. This is best accomplished by guiding the discussion toward a biblical perspective while drawing out the kids' own interpretations. In the end, however, if God's perspective has not clearly been brought to light, there should always be a wrap-up so that kids have a foundation upon which to base their opinions.

When in doubt, listen. When I was in high school, we had a new leader in our youth group who was having a hard time breaking in with the guys. He was friendly and tried to talk when he saw us, but it seemed that every time he asked a question, his eyes would wander if we took too long to answer. Before long, all we ever said to him was, "Fine," "Good," or "Okay." We didn't want to talk to him because he didn't appear to care about our responses.

It takes no special ability to be a good listener, yet the most effective youth-ministry gift is listening. Anyone can learn how to listen, because listening is not so much a skill as it is a commitment—to caring enough about kids to give them our undivided attention when they speak. We can improve how we communicate that commitment, but listening is basically love and respect in action.

Listening is something we do with our bodies. The way we sit or stand when someone is talking tells them how interested we are in what they are sharing. Maintaining eye contact is essential. Whether we nod and smile with interest or impatiently stare until the person is finished speaking communicates volumes.

A good way to find out how we come across as listeners is to try this exercise. Get with two other people and have one person talk, one listen, and one observe. Then talk together about the experience, switch roles, and go through the process again. Try to help one another pick out any "blind spots" that they may not notice.

A practical reason for being a good listener is so we'll know what the kids are talking about when we have to jump in and clarify the direction the group is going! As the facilitator, we are often the bridge from point to point, so we must stay closely in tune with the things that have been said.

Some Closing Tips

Here are twelve practical tips to leading great discussions:
1. Sit in a circle with everyone at eye level.
2. When calling on someone to share, call them by name.
3. Provide the opportunity for everyone to share without forcing anyone.
4. Avoid taking sides (or even revealing your opinion), especially early in a discussion.
5. Get the group to see you as a facilitator and not as the supreme authority.
6. Keep any one individual from monopolizing or controlling the discussion.
7. Humor has its place, so maintain a balance—not too much to be disruptive, but not so stiff that kids don't enjoy themselves.
8. Know when to cut off a discussion.
9. Avoid leaving them with easy answers that don't relate to their world.

10. Avoid excessive harshness when you're injecting tension into a discussion.
11. Don't resolve every issue that comes up.
12. Give them something concrete to take with them after every discussion. ◆

APPENDIX **D**

Camping Ministry for 6th–8th Graders

Stan Beard
Director of Ministry Resources
Young Life

Excerpts taken from *Reaching Out to Early Adolescents: Junior High Ministry Handbook* by Stan Beard. Copyright © 1990 Young Life, pp. 15–19.

Camping has as profound and positive an impact on junior-high young people as it has on high-school kids. It is not too early to provide them with an experience of adventure and inspiration away from their normal environment. Planning weekend or week-long trips for kids where the Gospel is proclaimed and lived is one of the best things we can do with early adolescents. We must, however, carefully consider how we program these experiences, making sure we are not simply duplicating a program we have used many times with high school kids.

Recently I attended a weekend camp for sixth-, seventh-, and eighth-grade kids. The property was in perfect condition, the weather ideal, and the camp full with more than 300 excited kids. Everything pointed toward a fantastic experience of sharing Christ with kids in this excellent setting. Counselors, club leaders, and parents had worked very hard in training, preparing, and paying for this weekend event. Everything seemed to be ready except the camp staff who would be leading the kids!

From the beginning it was stated that the program would be an exact duplicate of the one used with high school kids several weeks earlier. Events, times, meals, meetings—nothing changed; everything was the same as when sixteen- through nineteen-year-old kids were there! Simple, effective, easy—let's run it through again! It worked with high-school kids, why not expect it to work with junior-high kids?

Are we too busy to make the necessary changes when a different age group comes along? Do we not know the developmental differences that are so evident? Have we forgotten our own affirmation "to meet kids where they are and minister to them at their level, not ours?" Are we really interested in relationships, or are we in fact Christian program directors?

I know these are hard questions, but we must wrestle with them if we are going to seriously answer the question of how to effectively do a camping ministry with young teenagers. Many things we do with high-school kids adapt naturally to junior-high kids—but some do not. We must learn the differences and try hard to hit the target developmentally and stay true to our calling of meeting and loving kids "where they are at" regarding their age, social, and ethnic backgrounds, and all the other realities of their lives.

Listed below are some of the things to consider when directing a camping experience with kids who are twelve- to fourteen-years-old. This list is incomplete and very general in nature, but it will give you some guidelines to think about when planning your program.

1. *Food.* Keep the meals basic! Prepare menu items you know and have tasted many times before. Junior high kids do not like to be surprised with new recipes or impressive presentations of "adult food." Obviously nutrition is a central factor, but do not worry about preparing the fancy casserole or the eye-catching vegetable dish. Junior-high kids will not be wowed and probably will not eat it. Meals with junior-high kids should be short (they

are not there for casual dinner conversation), wholesome, and tasty!

2. *Rules.* Program directors trying to make their way with joking around about "no rules, only strong suggestions" may be misunderstood by a large number of junior-high campers. Many of them still think in a very concrete way and will not pick up on the subtle humor that works so well with high-school kids. One junior high kid "learned to smoke" while at camp because the announcer said we did not care *if* kids smoked, only *where* they smoked. This young kid read this as *permission*!

   Make rules basic and clear. This does not have to be done in a negative or heavy-handed way, but save the humor and subtleties for somewhere else in the program. Junior-high kids usually are very good at taking directions, so this can be handled easily if we talk with them in specific terms.

   Something else to consider: junior-high kids are still in the early formation process of making value decisions regarding the patterns and relationships in their lives. We can be of immense help to them if we make clear statements regarding the seriousness of drugs, smoking, alcohol, sex, etc. I am not suggesting that this is the place for sermonizing, but it is an opportunity for kids to know clearly what is illegal and unacceptable at camp.

3. *Schedule (Sleep!).* Believe it or not, junior-high kids actually need more sleep than their older brothers and sisters. It is counter-productive for us to push them until 1:00 or 2:00 in the morning, simply because now they are teenagers and they can stay up late! Allow approximately one more hour of sleep in your schedule than you would with a high school or college camp. The results for all (counselors included) will generally be positive.

4. *Cabin times (discussion with counselors and other kids in cabin).* This is one of the most misunderstood and most often violated aspects of camping programs with junior-high kids. Young teens are extremely impressionable at taking in truth and learning about the Gospel, but they are not yet capable of expressing feelings and

conversing meaningfully about spiritual issues. They often want to know what is right. Black-and-white concepts are natural to them. Cabin discussions most likely are question-and-answer sessions leaving inexperienced counselors frustrated and defeated.

We can make some major corrections in this area if we bring the proper development expectations to these important cabin times with kids.

a. Keep cabin discussions short; fifteen-to-thirty minutes is usually enough for junior-high kids. Pursue important things that have come out of the discussion in a one-on-one fashion. Do not prolong the cabin time simply because one or two kids are really "into it!" Long, meaningful cabin times usually are a need of the counselor rather than the camper.

b. Ask questions that make the kids the expert on the answer. Junior-high kids are experts on their opinions, experiences, perspectives, and feelings. They may not be right regarding facts, information, or the intent of others, but they know what is going on inside of them. They are not yet very articulate at expressing it, but they *are* experts on *themselves*! Questions with clear, "multiple choice" type answers often work well.

Use questions like, "What was your understanding of the point the speaker was trying to make?" "How did you feel when you had that experience?" "Tell me about the kind of relationship you have with your parents." "What kinds of thoughts do you have about God's love for you?" "Did you feel excitement, fear, confusion, or something else when the speaker told that story?"

These questions allow the kids to be squarely in charge of their answers. They will sense that we are not fishing for the "correct" response and will build bridges that will lead to deeper communication when the time and setting are right.

c. Require kids to listen to one another. Junior-high kids are masters at interruptions and put-downs. A good junior-high cabin time will have as its main ingredient, the process of kids talking *one at a time*. Teaching them to listen is an important skill for counselors to apply. It is quite often a good idea in a junior-high cabin-time situation for the counselor to direct questions to a specific individual (e.g., "Johnny, what do you think?" "Suzy, how did you feel?" instead of "Do any of you have a comment?"). This will enhance listening and usually allow for more control and respect.

d. Make cabin-time expectations realistic, not idealistic. Junior-high kids are just beginning to grapple with values, spiritual truths, and meaningful relationships. *They are not yet mature enough to make life-time commitments. We should emphasize God's commitment to them rather than push for their commitment to God.* Both are real and necessary, but a good junior-high cabin discussion will give ample room for the kids to be confused, uncertain, and mixed up. They need adult love and tolerance more than correct answers and deep spiritual insight. Powerful impact is taking place. Appropriate spiritual response will follow, gradually perhaps, but it will happen. Let us not force it all during a cabin time!

5. *Free time.* Because early adolescents have not yet figured out what they like, who to relate to, and what they want to do, big blocks of free time do not work as well as with older kids. Good counselors will know how to make use of non-program time, but generally speaking, it is better to have several planned (perhaps optional) activities to help junior high kids in their choosing processes. You do not have to schedule every minute; simply be aware that these kids look to our leadership rather than to their own creativity when wondering what to do next!

6. *Content and proclamation of the Gospel.* At no time in life is there a more impressionable moment for Christ to be proclaimed to kids. The process of separation from parents has begun. The beginning of value formation is in full gear; addictive and damaging habits have not been

established yet (for most); heroes and role models are eagerly sought after. This period is God's "best chance at a life."

But, as with other aspects of teenage development, we must not assume that the junior higher's capacity to respond is the same as that of a high-school kid. The difference is significant, and so the form of our proclamation should be different as well. Below are several thoughts in this regard.

a. Illustrations should be real and clear. Impressive analogies usually miss junior-high kids (i.e., God-shaped vacuum, the quarterback of your life, living water, etc.). They respond to real stories and real situations. Visual illustrations are excellent with this age group. Show them what you are saying (difference between plastic flowers and ones that are growing). Use illustrations with which they can readily identify—family, movies, music, sports, etc.

b. Proclaim God's truth—do not be preoccupied with detailed explanations. Junior-high kids will not press you on the meaning of the incarnation or how substitutionary atonement personally applies to them. They are not concerned so much with the origin of sin as they are with the consequences of it. Let some of the important doctrines and details of our faith be explored a little later in life. At this early stage they need to hear and know:

• God's creation (stewards of universe and people in his image, self concept)

• Humanity's fall (separation, division, lostness)

• God's revelation (Christ)

• God's action (cross/resurrection)

• God's family (response to Christ)

• God's goal (life of love, growth, service)

Short, one-point messages are the most effective. Ample time for communicating one point is usually ten-to-fifteen minutes. The need for a tight, rigid sequence of message development is not necessary with young teenagers.

c. Use of role play. This an effective communication tool with early adolescents if used correctly. Quite often the kind of role play productions we do at high-school camps are a bit confusing to junior-high kids. Instead of identifying with certain role players, junior-high kids respond by wanting to change them. "Why are you that way?" "Don't you know what you are doing?" "Why don't you become something else?" They do a lot of judging rather than evaluating the pros and cons of a particular role player's character.

This response is due to the fact that mentally their brains are still in the developmental stage and have not fully progressed to think in abstract, evaluative ways. Reality for many junior-high kids is still very concrete, very black and white, very specific.

We do them a disservice when we simply reproduce a role play setting from a high-school camp and forget to consider the junior-high level of experience and development. Role plays that involve life situations seem to work very well with early adolescents.

Have leaders act out real common experiences (family conflicts; school experiences; personal, ethical, or moral dilemmas; decision making; etc.). Then talk about how the particular elements of the situation seem to be on target with their developmental process. Role playing needs to be very clearly stated to junior-high kids. They are easily confused and often identify a person's role as to how and who that person really is. Work hard at telling kids this is a dramatic scene, not to be taken as fact!

Role playing is an excellent proclamation tool with young teenagers. Use it carefully and adapt your situations to their level of interest and reality.